FACING THE WOLF

FACING THE WOLF

Inside the Process of Deep Feeling Therapy

//

Theresa Sheppard Alexander

//

A DUTTON BOOK

DUTTON

Published by the Penguin Group
Penguin Books USA Inc., 375 Hudson Street, New York, New York 10014, U.S.A.
Penguin Books Ltd, 27 Wrights Lane, London W8 5TZ, England
Penguin Books Australia Ltd, Ringwood, Victoria, Australia
Penguin Books Canada Ltd, 10 Alcorn Avenue, Toronto, Ontario, Canada M4V 3B2
Penguin Books (N.Z.) Ltd, 182–190 Wairau Road, Auckland 10, New Zealand

Penguin Books Ltd, Registered Offices:
Harmondsworth, Middlesex, England

First published by Dutton, an imprint of Dutton Signet,
a division of Penguin Books USA Inc.
Distributed in Canada by McClelland & Stewart Inc.

First Printing, April, 1996
10   9   8   7   6   5   4   3   2   1

◪ REGISTERED TRADEMARK—MARCA REGISTRADA

LIBRARY OF CONGRESS CATALOGING-IN-PUBLICATION DATA:
Alexander, Theresa Sheppard.
    Facing the wolf: inside the process of deep feeling therapy/
Theresa Sheppard Alexander.
        p.   cm.
    ISBN 0-525-94060-X
    1. Primal therapy—Case studies.   2. Adult child abuse victims—Case
studies.   3. Alexander, Theresa Sheppard.   I. Title.
RC489.P67A44   1996
616.89'14—dc20   95-20525
                                                                                   CIP

Printed in the United States of America
Set in New Baskerville

Designed by Jesse Cohen

This work is dedicated to the memory of
HATTIE BOOKER PETERSON
and
ELLEN JANOV

ACKNOWLEDGMENTS

I would like to thank each and every one of my patients for sharing themselves, their fears, pains, joys, and growth with me. I thank them as well for trusting me with their deepest heart.

I would like to thank Alice Miller for the inspiration of her books.

My thanks also go to all who read and commented on this work while it was in progress: Naya Pennington and Wendy Campbell for efforts above and beyond the call of friendship; and Roger Rubin, Lisa Lancaster, Sarah Bellwood, Peter Bellwood, Jonathan Christie, Margaret Christie, Phillis Sheppard, Patricia Sheppard, Marietta Patricia Leis, Susanna Bluestein, Adele Kahn, Caroline Wood, Sherry Anderson, Carol Aronoff, and my husband, Michael Alexander. I also thank Ann Petersen Christie for telling me all those Danish proverbs.

Many thanks to all the members of my writing group for reading and commenting on this work: Tina Bachemin, Joseph Crawford, Susan Dormanen, Mark Nishimura, Ray Shine, Stacey Thoyre, Sophia Vinogradov, and Lisa Worthington.

Thanks to my son, Phillip, for understanding when I needed to write and for being a light and joy in my life.

And last but far from least I thank each one of my brothers and sisters for being my dearest allies, enemies, friends, playmates, and everything else siblings are to one another; but most of all I appreciate the gift of love you gave and allowed me to give to you. Only those who were there truly know.

CONTENTS

INTRODUCTION

"YOU CAN'T RUN FROM THE WOLF BECAUSE THE WOLF travels with you." This Danish proverb tells it truly. Slowly, over the years, it was borne in on me that the wolf of my childhood—my fear, pain, and rage—was always with me, always lurking, ready to pounce at any moment. Sometimes the wolf was wild and ravenous, raging and slashing at some small transgression on another's part. This would often happen with one of my younger brothers or sisters, or a person I was sure wouldn't harm me physically. At other times, this same wolf would cringe and be submissive at the very moment my strength and courage were required. This side of my wounded personality would emerge when I felt in conflict with a powerful authority figure, or when I was with people I very much wanted to like me.

Often, in these situations, I could not control what I did. I would yell fiercely at someone that I wasn't afraid of who made a small mistake but find myself meekly agreeing to rectify the much larger mistake that a frightening person had made. Looking back on my actions later, I would be consumed with shame or sadness. But I would do the very same thing again the next time. I would try to rise above the situation or the feelings only to find my inappropriate behavior seeping out in some other area of my life. I began to feel that I was trapped with this wolf, that he would be forever chasing me over the landscape of my life, a life that felt empty, stupid, and pointless.

I have written this book because I struggled for years to control, change, and deny the effects of my childhood. I thought that simply by growing up and leaving home I could escape the reality of the torment and sadness I had suffered there. What a horrible discovery it was to find that this was not possible.

A further consequence of years of having been a frightened, unloved child was the unbridgeable gap between my feelings, my mind, and my body. These splits in myself caused me to be very vulnerable to feelings of confusion, self-loathing, and fear. I was often filled with sadness over something that happened to me, while at the same time observing myself with a critical, unfeeling eye. I was once treated very rudely by a bus driver while I was visiting in the South. I trembled with rage at the driver while my throat was tight with tears. But I was also coldly observing my reactions and berating myself for getting on the bus at all, for asking the driver for directions, and for not having a clever reply to his rudeness. For months afterward whenever I thought of this incident my stomach would begin to hurt, while I sat in even the most ordinary circumstances, with a false appearance of ease. I trusted no one, not even myself, because I knew that I could turn against myself in a moment. I had no compassion for myself, except in extremely brief moments that I contemptuously labeled "feeling sorry for myself."

I had been told by many of my teachers that I was a very bright girl with a great deal of potential. I was a National Achievement Scholarship finalist and as such I had received scholarship offers from several colleges and universities. I entered a college in my hometown in the fall of 1967. I only managed to last in school for two weeks before I was overcome with anxiety and fear about my ability to do the work. I left without a word to anyone. I would periodically reenter school and take one course. I could not use my intellectual abilities in a full and meaningful way. I supported myself by doing menial, dead-end jobs. Still, I haunted my local library, reading everything I could about psychology and trying to understand what was wrong with me.

Then in May 1970, at the age of twenty, I had the good fortune to encounter *The Primal Scream,* a book by Arthur Janov, Ph.D. Somewhat taken aback by its grandiose claims, especially that therapy would only be a three-week process, I was nonetheless driven by the hope that some of what he wrote could be true. Eleven days after reading that book I was, through the generosity of Arthur and Vivian Janov, a patient in Primal Therapy. It was during this therapy, through the profound effect of confronting the trauma and pain I suffered in my childhood, that I was able to heal and grow to an extent that I had not imagined possible. Of course, the process of this therapy lasted far longer than three weeks.

After several years in therapy, equipped with a stronger sense of myself and feeling more confident and happy, I was able to continue my education, receiving my B.A. and M.A. degrees. I also entered the training program at the Primal Institute in Los Angeles and five years later earned my certificate as a Primal therapist. I worked for the Primal Institute for several years after that. As I became more experienced, I began to train and supervise trainee therapists in the Institute's training program. Eventually I became the resident director of the Institute in New York City. In 1981 I left the Institute and developed a private practice in New York. I now live and work in Northern California.

This is the story of my original encounter with my own

deepest feelings. Although the details are unique to me, I believe many of the insights and realizations to be relevant for others as well. The first part of the book comprises the sessions, reported as clearly as my memories and extensive diaries allow. They are presented from alternating perspectives: that of the patient, which I was at first, and then that of a therapist, which I later became. The second part of the book presents the more technical aspects of Deep Feeling work. In my diaries and memories, my own thoughts and feelings are very clear, and are reported almost verbatim. Since my first therapist during the "intensive" phase of my therapy, Ellen Janov, died very tragically in a house fire many years ago, I was not able to consult with her as I wrote this book. Consequently, the voice, thoughts, and perceptions of the therapist are mine, based on how I do Deep Feeling therapy now.

I chose to use actual sessions and events from my own therapy, and to compose the therapist's reactions and interventions from my own experience as a therapist, for two reasons. First, though I considered using sessions with some of my own patients to illustrate this form of therapy from the therapist's view, I wanted to be certain there would be no regrets at the secrets revealed. After deep thought and discussions with a respected older colleague, I concluded that only by using my own story could I be sure I was not breaching my patients' boundaries. So I chose to reveal my own secrets, rather than those of others. Second, since my therapist is dead, I was absolutely prevented from using her as a resource in reconstructing her part of our journey together. Because dialogue is the format that best teaches how this work is done, I felt compelled to use the knowledge of the only other person in that room when my therapy took place, myself.

My further purpose in presenting the therapy sessions in dialogue form is to demystify the process of going into deep feelings. Though in recent years several therapists and psychotherapy practitioners have begun to write about the benefits of confronting and entering one's deep feelings, no one to my knowledge has presented the process as it happens moment to moment. In writing the book in this manner, my intention is to show the *inner process* of moments of deep feeling.

By reading and experiencing my account of this healing process, others who suffer as I did may recognize the benefit of having the courage to confront their own painful and traumatic past.

A childhood of abuse is not erased by reaching adulthood. Nor can it be forgotten or ignored. Some of its effects can be lessened and some of its pain eased by the verbal discussions, intellectual understanding, awareness of deep feelings, and connected relationship utilized by conventional psychotherapies. But I strongly believe that for some of us, especially those most severely wounded, true growth and healing can only take place through confronting and feeling those most awful memories that still lurk in the crevasses of the mind and heart. Denial cannot take the pain away, but mourning and insight can bring healing.

My own early experience in therapy at age twenty had a profound and lasting effect. Of course I wasn't "cured" in those short weeks of my initial intensive, as I had so naively hoped, but I was on the path to recovery. I had begun to turn and face my wolf instead of trying to run away. Over time there was a change in the way I felt about myself, as well as a change in the way I chose to conduct my life. The key concept here is choice. Until I began to confront my pain and its resultant and continuing damage, I rarely felt I *had* a choice.

Driven by my needs and fears, I continually behaved in certain ways because I felt forced to do so and in effect sabotaged myself. This behavior and many other aspects of my personality, interaction with myself, other people, and the world changed as a result of confronting my deepest feelings and fears. Now I know I was not alone in enduring those feelings, but at the time I thought that no one else struggled with these issues. I believe that others can benefit from facing the wolf—that they, also, can become people with choices.

In more than twenty years of practice I have worked with people from many countries and cultures and learned my childhood story is not unique. Child abuse and neglect are not confined to the citizens of any one country or economic stratum, nor to those who practice any particular religion. I hope my book will ultimately help to lessen the pain children suffer in our society, since it is my belief that when adults allow themselves to confront the past memories of their own painful childhoods, they will no longer be insensitive to the needs and feelings of children in the present.

I offer this work as a beacon of hope to those still suffering the long-term effects of childhood pain. You *can* heal.

—Theresa Sheppard Alexander
May 1995

AUTHOR'S NOTE

In the context of this book the terms *feeling,*
having a feeling, feeling a feeling, and *connected feeling*
have a very specific meaning. To me, these terms
mean a connected, total descent into the emotional
reality of a past traumatic event. The patient returns
to the moment of trauma and "feels" the emotion of
that time, which was too painful or frightening to
fully experience when it occurred. By "connected" I
mean there is a definite awareness of what the past
trauma was and also a clear sense of the activating
event in the present, if any. Many sessions begin without this clarity of perception, but with access to
deeper levels of feeling, understanding does come.

PART I

Deep Feeling Therapy
in Practice

Session One

The Patient Speaks

IT WAS CLEAR TO ME EARLY IN LIFE THAT SOME-
thing was wrong in my family. I was certain that it
wasn't all right for my father to beat us so often or so
very hard. After his beatings we children would
gather together and examine our welts and bruises.
We'd cry and try to comfort one another. We promised one another we would never, ever treat *our* children this way. Sometimes my mother would argue
fiercely with my father about his beating us; but other
times she would be the one who instigated the beating. I never knew for sure which way she would turn.

I desperately wanted to know what was wrong
with my parents, but even more I wanted to know
what was wrong with *me*. My brothers and sisters were
often able to laugh and play; but I never seemed to

fit in with other children. I was often afraid and shy. I didn't feel free to run and play the way others my age seemed to. I felt I had to sit still, be quiet, not cause trouble. I was meant to *help*, not *cause trouble*.

I recall many instances in my life of needing help and being too afraid and ashamed to ask. The long tentacles of this feeling were revealed to me shortly after my own feeling work began. One powerful memory was of getting lost in the subway and bus system of my hometown one day after school. I couldn't ask anyone—not a bus conductor or anyone with a friendly face—for directions. Why? The therapy session that follows answers this question. Since Primal feelings relate to specifics—specific memories and incidents that have a lasting effect on a child's perception of herself and the world—what follows is most minutely reported.

As with most people who spent childhood feeling unwanted and unloved, I entered the therapy room checking for signs that my therapist either hated or loved me; I took the slightest shift in her attention as a sure sign of being hated or unwanted. A smile or lightening of the eyes relieved me and made me feel safe for a few moments.

On this particular day my therapist seemed pensive and was not smiling. I got scared. After a bit of silence, she asked, "How are you?"

"Oh, I'm fine," I replied in a bright, cheerful voice.
SILENCE
"Really fine or polite fine?" she questioned quietly.

"Polite," I said, a little less brightly.

"Why don't you tell me how you really are?"

A moment of crisis! Could I really say that I was afraid of her? That I was sure she didn't like me? That I was certain she wished she could get out of this room and go have fun in the California sunshine? Of course not. I lied.

"Oh, I'm just a bit nervous."

SILENCE

I filled in the silence with thinking that SHE thought I was an idiot, that she was wondering how she had got such a hard and stupid patient, and that she knew I had lied.

" 'Nervous.' What does that mean?"

Uh-oh. I could feel her closing in on me. Now I wanted to get out of this room.

"You know—butterflies in your stomach, your heart beating faster—that kind of stuff."

"No, I don't know what it's like for you. Tell me."

"Well, nervous is when you're a little scared."

"And you're scared now?"

"Anxious, maybe."

"What is it that's making you nervous and scared and anxious?"

I still could not say, "I am afraid that you don't like me and don't want to be here." So I got a little bit closer to the truth, but still didn't tell it. "Being here, I guess," I mumbled.

"What about being here does that to you?"

SILENCE

5

My mind scurried around, trying to think. I was afraid of her, I was afraid she didn't like me, I was afraid to tell her I was afraid, and I was afraid that I was doing this wrong. "I miss my home." Telling a truth, but not *the* truth.

"Oh," she said. "Is it hard being so far from home?" Her voice sounded gentle.

"I want to go home." Tears came to my eyes and I put my hand over my mouth, pressing on my lips. I was afraid to make any noise. Then my feeling stumbled to a stop. I was confused. "I don't know what happened. I don't know what I'm crying about."

"You cried when you said, 'I want to go home.' "

Tears sprang to my eyes again as I said, "I want to go home." I cried for a few seconds, then stopped once more.

Silence reigned.

"I don't know what to do now."

"Let yourself keep saying it," my therapist told me.

"I want to go home. . . . I want to go home."

Nothing happened.

"What were you thinking of when you first cried?" she asked.

I immediately felt sad again as I remembered the yellow mailbox in front of my house, the yellow mailbox that was three thousand miles away in another state, since I was in Los Angeles having my three-week intensive. "I feel so far away from home. I don't know when I'll get there again or when I'll see my boyfriend."

I was crying in earnest now, tears pouring down my face. I still spoke very softly; no sounds of crying escaped my lips. My mind started to drift as I thought of my boyfriend. I didn't feel bad when I thought of him. Then my mind's eye homed in on the yellow mailbox again, and I fell into sadness. Somehow, that mailbox meant home. "I want to go home," I said again and again, with the image of the mailbox in my inner eye. After crying very softly for about ten minutes, I stopped, blowing my nose and telling my therapist about the importance of the yellow mailbox, that it meant home.

"Yes," she said, "you'll find that there is usually one visual image or one phrase that keeps you connected to your feeling. It hurts more when you think of it. If you allow yourself to go in the direction of where it hurts, that is following the feeling. Is there anything else that you thought of or remembered as you were crying?"

"Yes, I thought of why home is so important. It's because at home you can get help."

"And are you feeling the need for help now?" my therapist asked. I felt a thrill of fear. She was getting very close. Somehow it didn't seem so hard to tell her the truth this time. "I am, and it makes me very afraid. I have the feeling that you don't like me and that you don't want to have to help me." I sneaked a quick look at her face. She didn't look angry, which is what I was expecting.

"Why wouldn't I want to help you?"

"I don't know."

There was a long pause. As the moments trickled by, I found myself feeling more and more miserable; a heavy feeling sat high in my chest, and my nose and throat felt thick. As the time passed I began to feel very sad. Why wouldn't she want to help me? It just didn't seem possible that she would.

"Do you want me to help you?"

Another long pause, as I again found it very hard to admit.

"Yes."

"Ask me." Her voice sounded friendly.

In my mind, my voice was shouting *"Help me!"* but when I finally spoke, I didn't say it like that. "Help me," I said, very quietly, then, "Nobody wants to help me."

As I said those words, I burst out crying. Tears poured from my eyes. I was very quiet, as always, but it was hard to stay that way. The sadness was so intense that my chest felt fit to burst. But what I'd said was the truth. Nobody wanted to help me. I knew it. I was completely certain of it. I turned on my side on the couch and cried and cried, thinking, "Nobody wants to help me." I was wracked by sobs. My therapist remained quiet. Then I thought, "Why doesn't anyone want to help me? Why? Why? Why?"

As I cried I felt more and more alone, more and more unwanted. At first I kept thinking of my therapist and wanting her to help me, to *want* to help me. My heart ached. I started saying, "My heart hurts."

Each time I repeated the phrase my heart seemed to hurt me more. Suddenly, there was a shift of what I saw in my mind's eye. For some reason I thought of my father. It was such a surprise that my crying ground to a halt. Why was I thinking of him?

I reached for some tissues from a box nearby. I blew my nose repeatedly, stunned that so much mucus could come from my body. As I lay there, quietly thinking back over what had just happened, I could hardly believe that I'd said those things to my therapist, that I'd really let her know what I felt.

I was quiet for quite a long time. Then I became conscious that my therapist was still sitting there. I turned to her and said, "I suddenly thought of my father, I don't even know why." She didn't say anything for a bit and then she asked what I'd thought about him.

I went into an internal downward spiral, my mind winding back to the moment when he popped into my mind. I could see his face clearly, looking very cool and uninterested. My father was very good-looking, but he wasn't looking good here. I told my therapist that I could see him and that he looked so cold and uncaring. "How do you feel when you see his face like that?" she asked me. As I let myself see him again in my mind's eye, I got a sinking, heavy feeling in the middle of my chest. I soon recognized what the feeling was. I felt sad, very sad. I reported that to her. We were silent for a long time. As the quiet continued I

could feel myself getting sadder and sadder, though I
didn't know why.

"When have you seen that look on your father's
face?" The therapist's voice was suddenly inserted into
my reverie. With that question, I felt my heart take a
dive into deeper, blacker sadness. I suddenly felt confused and overwhelmed by the images from my childhood flashing through my mind's eye. Scenes were
whipping by—riding in the car, standing in the
kitchen, or outside in the garden—then everything
slowed down and the focus narrowed in onto my father's face.

It was as if a door had opened into the past. My
father was standing on the front porch of our house
as I limped home supported by my younger brother.
He had a pot in his hands and was calmly drying it
with a kitchen towel. I looked up as I got to the bottom of the porch steps and saw that look on his face.
I began to tell my therapist what I'd remembered,
bursting into tears with the words, "He wouldn't
come get me."

My whole body and feelings were catapulted back
to that summer day just before my twelfth birthday. It
had begun with excitement and happy anticipation.
This was the day of the annual picnic for the altar
boys and choir girls from my parochial school. We
were all being rewarded for our year of faithful service with a free trip to Palisades Park in New Jersey!
My brother Arthur and I were going together, as
he was an altar boy. We were up and dressed long be-

fore we needed to be and charged out the front door with my mother's "Have a good time and be careful" echoing in our ears. We skipped and ran on our way to school, where we would take chartered buses to the amusement park.

This was the one day of the year that the sisters didn't make us behave ourselves. We laughed and played on the buses, and the nuns themselves were having a good time with us, teasing and joking. When we eventually arrived at Palisades Park, our spirits were at a fever pitch of excitement. We stayed on the bus for a few minutes as we received our assignments: each nun would have ten of us in her charge and we were strictly ordered to stay with our assigned sister and not get lost. With a final instruction about meeting back near the picnic tables to eat our lunch, we were released from the bus. Within minutes, the buses left. They'd be back at four to take us home.

Wild with excitement, we began playing in the picnic area even before we got to any of the rides. Laughing and giggling, we ran around in circles as the sisters were setting up the coolers with our food on the tables. I was playing a fast game of chase with some of my friends from choir when I was stopped in my tracks by excruciating pain. My foot was sticking to a wooden board. A nail had pierced through my shoe and was embedded deep in my right foot. I screamed with pain and was soon surrounded by nuns and children. Looking at my foot made me feel sick and dizzy—the board was still sticking to it. With a quick motion I jerked my foot free. Then all the strength went out of me, and one sister helped me to a seat. I felt weak and afraid. More than anything, I wanted to go home. This presented a dilemma, since the buses had already left and there was no way for me to get home. Sister Michael Andrew cleaned the wound and got bandages from somewhere. There was no getting away from the pain, though; I was in agony. It was only ten o'clock and there were six more hours to get through until we could leave. Although my foot hurt fiercely, I very much wanted to go on the rides with the other children, and the sisters agreed to let me try to get around with them. It wasn't so bad at the beginning, but as the day passed my foot hurt more and more.

I cried a few times, but generally tried to be brave. Everyone was very sweet to me, and one of the choir girls who was much bigger than I carried me for a while. Finally, about two o'clock, I just had to go sit down; I'd been hopping about on one leg and was exhausted as well as in pain. I sat with one of the sisters at the picnic tables. As I sat there, though, I couldn't stay still, for my foot throbbed and burned no matter what position I tried. I consoled myself with thoughts of home and my parents, who would make it all better.

Eventually the buses arrived and we started toward the school. The nuns tried to arrange for the bus driver to drop me off at home, but that didn't work out; there was something about him following an arranged route and it not being possible for him to deviate from it. The final arrangement was that he would drop me off on my street, but several blocks from my house.

By that time, I couldn't put my little pink shoe back on. When I tried, it hurt so much that my stomach turned over. Arthur, shorter than me and just as scared, helped me from the bus. I bent my foot back, like a flamingo, and started hopping, one-legged, down the street.

It was still a beautiful day and the smell of the flowers from all the gardens wafted toward us in the cooling evening air. My brother and I tried to joke about how funny we looked hopping down the street, but we couldn't really laugh. I was in too much pain. My foot felt swollen and hot. It throbbed and chattered with pain. Each hop jarred it again and again. I could feel the pulse of my blood through my entire foot, and what it pulsed was pain. It was too much for me to bear. I started crying. "Please go home and get Daddy. It hurts too much now," I said. My brother started running home.

I sat down to wait on the stone retaining wall of a neighbor's garden. I couldn't stop crying at first, but slowly the pain lessened as I sat still. I kept looking down the street, waiting to see my father's tall form coming to rescue me. Twice I saw men walking toward me in the distance and relaxed into the thought of my father's strong arms carrying me the rest of the way home. Both times my heart leapt up, then crashed as the man got closer and I saw he was a stranger. Finally I saw my brother Hubert—who was a little taller and stronger than Arthur—trudging up the street toward me. He came and stood very close to me and, looking me in the eye, he sadly said, "Daddy said, 'Come home.' "

I was stunned. How could I get there without his help? However, I'd been ordered home in the military tone of voice that my father used when he meant business, and I knew I had to go. With my brother's help and after several stops along the way I finally got to the steps leading to our porch. There, I looked up and saw Daddy's face.

I cried the entire time I poured out this story to my therapist. The tale didn't come out in one clear paragraph either. There were many, many stops as I cried and cried and pieced together the story of my father refusing to help me. I cried the hardest at two spots. I knew it was important to tell her these because she had strongly emphasized in an earlier session the importance of these "hot spots," places that caused me the most intense pain and sadness. The first was as I sat on the wall waiting for Daddy to come and saw my younger brother walking toward me. "He's not coming to get me. He doesn't care that I'm hurt," I sobbed. And then, with strong encouragement from my therapist to "let it out, let yourself say everything," I began begging and pleading in my feeling. "Daddy, please come, please, please, please, I really need you now. I've tried to be brave, but it hurts too much."

All through these words, I was sobbing and crying in torment and disbelief. How could he not have come when I needed him so desperately? The pain inside was like a black hole, sucking everything else into it, leaving nothing but pain. I found myself biting my lip and holding my breath to try to make the hurting stop.

Suddenly, my therapist was right beside me, crouched down on the floor, not touching but very close. Her voice was soft but very intense: "You don't have to keep it inside anymore. Let the feeling out *now*." The dam burst. I began shrieking, "Help me! Help me, help, help, help, help, please help me. I'm your little girl. Don't you care? I'm your little daughter. I'm waiting, and I need you. Help, help, help, help. It hurts me. It hurts. It hurts. I'm hurting. I'm hurting. I hurt. I need. I hurt."

Finally I had nothing more to say and cried on and on without words as it sank in that my father hadn't cared enough about me to come and see how badly I was hurt. After what seemed forever but was actually about twenty minutes, the sobbing and the sadness died down. As I recovered from the feeling, I remember being astonished at the details of my memories. The feel of the stone wall pressing into the back of my legs, the shadow of my own body on the sidewalk, the smell of the flowers in the garden all came back to me as I went deep into my feeling. As my awareness shifted back into the present, I became aware of my therapist again. We were both quiet for quite some time and then I said to her, "He didn't even come to see how badly I was hurt."

"Your own father refused to come help you. Unbelievable," was her reply. Her voice sounded sad and sympathetic and seemed to echo the sadness I had felt. Then she asked, "What happened when you did get home?" As I recounted the slow, hopping progress I made down the street to our house, I could feel myself getting sad again. It sank in deeper and deeper that at my time of most desperate need, my father, my one and only father, couldn't be bothered to help me, didn't even want to help me.

My father's look stayed with me as I let my memories roll back through the years. After I got home, Daddy turned and walked into the house before I got up the steps. My mother had been in the kitchen, and as I later found out, was unaware that I'd been hurt or that I had sent for help. She rushed out of the kitchen and immediately removed the bandages from my foot and questioned me about what had happened. "It's a deep puncture," she said. "We'll have to take you to the hospital emergency room for a tetanus shot."

My father immediately said, "Hospital? *I* never went to the hospital when *I* stepped on a nail." Then he picked up my foot, looked at the hole in it, and quickly dropped my foot with a snort of disgust. "That doesn't look very serious to me."

"Whether it looks serious to you or not, it is,"

my mother insisted. "Let's get the car and take her right away."

"I'm not driving her to the hospital and that's final."

Mother tried again. "Give me the keys and I'll drive," she said.

"I said *no* and I meant it!" With that, Daddy stormed out of the room. My mother eventually borrowed crutches from a neighbor and took me on the hour-long public transportation ride to the hospital.

Telling my therapist all this, I felt sad and angry, but just too tired from my earlier bouts of feeling to go more deeply into it. It would be more of the same. He didn't want to help me and didn't want anyone else to help me either. I cried a bit more, and then silence fell between us. I was thinking over the session, that it had been so hard to tell her I was afraid and that I needed help. Now I told her how I'd lied at the beginning, that I'd been too afraid to tell her the whole truth. It was so very clear now: if my own father refused to help me, how could I possibly believe that a stranger—even my therapist—would do so? He had left me ashamed of myself, certain that I wasn't worthy of being helped.

"Is that what made it so hard for you to tell me that you wanted me to help you?" she questioned.

"Definitely," I answered. "I couldn't risk ever seeing that look on someone's face again. And I was completely sure that you didn't want to help me either."

"How do you feel about me wanting to help you now?"

"It seems almost possible."

"It will get more possible," she said with a smile. "When are the other times you remember needing help?" she asked.

I immediately recalled getting lost in the bus and subway system of my town. I had spent hours wandering, looking and hoping to find my own way. I thought of asking for help; but I just could not do it. I was too afraid. Now I knew that I had been afraid—no, certain—of being refused. Next I told her of my feelings as a student. If I didn't understand something in the classroom, I never asked for further explanation, just pretended that all was well. Then I thought of my relationship with my boyfriend and began to tell her of my feeling of needing to be completely independent. I never wanted to need anything from him and would try with all my might to do anything and everything for myself. There were also times when I thought he should know I needed help without my having to ask, and I'd get angry that he didn't.

"Are there any other ways this feeling has affected you?" was her next question. My younger brothers and sisters came to mind immediately. If any one of them asked me for anything I would move heaven and earth to try to get it for them. I could not stand the thought of them needing something and not getting it. I didn't want them to feel as I had felt on that long ago summer day, and I didn't want to feel it myself through seeing them suffer. I suddenly realized that I didn't even know if I *wanted* to help them; I just couldn't stand the idea of not helping them.

My therapist explained to me that this problem wasn't magically cured now, from having experienced this one feeling, that it would still be hard for me to ask for help at times, but that it would become more and more possible, over time. After some more talk we agreed on the time for our session the next day, and I left.

Looking at my watch while I walked outside afterward, I could hardly believe that more than two hours had passed. I felt light and carefree. The sun seemed to be shining brighter; smells were more intense and my body glowed with energy. I felt like kicking up my heels and running. I felt happy! Was it really possible to feel happy after experiencing all that pain and sadness? Evidently it was.

Session Two

The Patient Speaks

THAT EVENING, AS I SAT IN MY MOTEL ROOM RE-
membering that day's session, I kept thinking over
and over, "How could Daddy not come to help me?
How could he?" The only answer seemed to be that
he didn't love me and didn't care enough about me.
I started wondering about what would happen in the
next session. Would I continue talking about Daddy?
Or maybe feel the rest of what happened that day? I
couldn't really tell. I didn't have anything to do to
distract myself from thoughts about therapy or my
feelings. By the rules of the Institute, I wasn't supposed to watch television or read or listen to music or
exercise when I wasn't in session. These were all of
my "act outs"—activities I used to distract and protect
myself from my feelings—and they were specifically

prohibited during the three-week intensive. Nor was I allowed to call people on the telephone. What to do? I thought about my childhood until I was sick of thinking about it. Then I bathed and brushed my teeth and finally went to bed.

As I lay in bed trying to go to sleep I suddenly became convinced that there was someone in the closet. I was terrified. Then my rational side took over. Of course there wasn't anyone in that closet. Cursing myself for being an idiot, I nevertheless got out of bed and tiptoed over to the closet door. Standing to the side, in case someone ran out, I whipped it open quickly. Relief! Of course there was no one there. I ran back to bed and jumped in. Thinking about the incident, I remembered an under-the-stairs closet in my childhood home that had been terrifying to me as I was growing up. At night I was afraid to walk past it and would try to jump past the open space in order to get to the staircase. Reminding myself to tell my therapist about this in the morning, I fell asleep.

I woke up screaming. I'd been trapped in a nightmare, one I remembered from childhood. Giant, carnivorous, space-creature wolves had been chasing me, ready to eat me alive. After running with all my might to escape, I'd finally been cornered at an impenetrable hedge in a deep, dark forest. I woke just as the wolves were launching themselves at me, ready to feed. I didn't know what had wakened me—the point I'd reached in the dream or the sound of my own screams. I found myself sitting bolt upright in the bed. At first I didn't know where I was, but I soon reoriented myself: I was in California, in a motel, and I was in Primal Therapy. Still gasping, I slowly lowered myself back onto the bed. After lying there for a few minutes I turned on the light and checked the time. It was three-thirty in the morning, still a long time to go before my session. I lay there for a bit staring at the ceiling, then turned off the light and tried to sleep. Of course I couldn't. I tossed this way and then that way, arranging and rearranging my pillows. Finally, in the middle of a fantasy about chocolate chip cookies and milk, I fell asleep again.

When I wakened in the morning my nightmare and my fear seemed very far away. I felt cool, calm, and collected. After having a shower and getting dressed, I left the room, heading for a nearby coffee shop for breakfast. Since the rules for the intensive stated no stimulants such as coffee, so there would be no artificial alteration of one's emotional state, I went without that morning staple drink and had milk instead. I found myself not feeling very hungry and left most of the food on my plate. With nothing to do until my session, I went back to the motel room and thought about my dream, wondering what would happen next in therapy.

I started off for my session with time to spare. It was another sunny Los Angeles day, and I wandered along the street, noticing the cars and occasionally speaking to someone that I passed. As I walked I noticed a woman I thought of as looking "motherly" coming toward me. As we passed each other I looked at her and with a smile said, "Hello." She completely ignored me, though it was more than that. She saw me, but she chose to look through me. I walked on with a pain like a railroad spike in the middle of my chest.

My therapist opened the door to her office when I arrived, and after we both had settled she asked, "And how are you today?"

"Not very well," was my reply.

I tried marshaling my thoughts. Where should I begin? With the woman on the street, the space wolf nightmare, or my fright before falling asleep? Then I noticed how worried I was that she would be angry that I didn't know where to begin. "I'm not sure exactly where to start," I said.

"You mentioned that you aren't doing very well; what's the matter?" She didn't seem to be angry. That encouraged me to try to really tell her.

"Well, I got really scared alone in the room last night, then I had a nightmare, and my feelings got hurt on the way here now. They all feel important to me, but I'm not sure which is most important."

"A good way to get a sense of that is to let yourself think about all those different incidents, let yourself see them internally and then notice which one has the most emotional charge. Which is the most sad, or most frightening, or the one that makes you the most angry. Take some time and check inside yourself."

I did as she suggested, feeling myself gravitating toward the incident with the woman on the street. I felt sad and hurt each time I saw the moment that she had looked right through me. How could she do that? But even as I was about to tell her about the woman, I could feel myself shrinking from doing so.

"I feel really shy about telling you," I said to her.

There was a moment of silence before she gently asked me, "What is that about?"

I thought briefly, and it came to me. "I'm afraid you'll think I'm a whiner and a crybaby."

"A whiner and a crybaby?"

"Yes, because it was very trivial, and I shouldn't let things like this bother me."

"If it bothers you or hurts you, it can't really be that trivial, can it? Tell me what happened."

Feeling in some small way reassured, I began to tell her.

"It was only a moment but it hurt me so much. I was on the way here and not feeling bad. The sun was shining and I was noticing the different kinds of cars and people on the street. An older woman was walking toward me and as we got close to each other, I said, 'Hello.' She looked right through me and walked past." I could feel myself choking up as I told her.

SILENCE

"Say what you're thinking."

"How could she be so mean? I was just being polite." I could feel my throat getting tighter and tighter. "It really hurt my feelings. What could be wrong with her speaking back to me? I don't understand." I stopped speaking and stared at the ceiling, then buried myself in the corner of the sofa and hid my face. Somehow I just couldn't let my therapist see me. I didn't want anyone to see my sadness. Again I had that feeling of a railroad spike in the middle of my chest. It wasn't physical pain, but the hurt was so deep it felt physical, like something really heavy pressing onto my chest. Each time I saw that woman's face looking toward me but through me I wanted to hide more. I felt small and worthless and dirty. My thoughts trailed off into nothingness, but still I had that pain in my chest. After being quiet for a while I started wondering out loud, "What makes that feel so bad?"

"What do you mean?" my therapist asked.

"Each time I thought of that woman looking through me it made me feel worse and worse. I don't understand how a person I'll never see again could hurt me so much."

"It probably has a lot to do with something in your past," she said. "Does this seem familiar?"

"I was wondering about this as I was lying here, wondering if it has to do with my feeling about Daddy yesterday, but somehow it seems different."

"What is the difference?"

I thought about it for a moment and then it hit me. "In the feeling yesterday with my father, I wanted something. I needed him to care about me and help me. With this woman I wasn't feeling that I needed anything from her; in fact, I thought I was giving something."

"That's certainly not how she responded, was it?"

"No," I replied, as the sadness hit me again.

"What hurts?"

"That I'm being nice and giving and it's being thrown back in my face. It makes me feel small and dirty, that what I'm giving is worthless and I'm worthless, too." Fierce, hot tears started to gather in the corners of my eyes.

"Are you really worthless?" she asked me very gently.

"I know I'm not, but it hurts so much that it feels true."

"Tell her how much she hurt you."

"It feels really silly." I didn't want to do it. I wanted to get out of this, to go somewhere else. I started squirming and turning.

"Stay with the pain. Don't run away. *Tell her.*"

I felt stuck between a rock and a hard spot. "I don't want to tell her anything."

"What don't you want to tell her?"

"I don't want to tell her she hurt me." My throat felt gripped in a vise, my lips pressed tightly together, my eyes burning.

"That's the feeling!" The therapist's voice dropped, becoming extremely intense. "Tell her now!"

"You hurt me," I muttered. I didn't want to do this. I felt like a fool.

"Again!"

"You hurt me." This time I mumbled.

"Again, louder!" Her voice had risen.

"You hurt me." A little volcano started rumbling in my chest.

"Shout it out!"

"You hurt me! You hurt me! You hurt me!" I broke down into sobs. Hot, burning tears popped from my eyes like pellets. Then more words came: "You make me feel so bad, please don't hurt me. You're hurting me. You're hurting me. You're hurting me!" By now I was shouting with all my might; and then I lost all words as I cried.

Suddenly, I wasn't thinking about that nameless woman on Sunset Boulevard. I was far away in space and time, walking my friend Coleen Calahan home. Our cat had had kittens and Coleen was taking one home. My mother had sent me along to carry her bookbag, since Coleen was carrying the kitten. I'd never been to her house, though we talked every day at school and I knew her twin brother, who was also in our class. I was looking forward to meeting her mother. As we walked along, Coleen kept telling me not to bother to come all the way home with her, that she could carry her books herself. I insisted; Mother told me to carry her books home for her and that was what I was going to do. Coleen got more and more nervous, which I assumed was because she didn't want me to go to any trouble. Finally, she stopped walking and turned to me. Her face turned bright red and her blond hair was blowing all around her face in the March wind. She looked me in the eye, then at the ground. "You can't come to my house," she mumbled, her words almost blowing away in the wind. I barely heard her, and I didn't believe it anyway. "What?" I almost shouted, trying to get the word out over the dread I felt in my stomach and the pounding of my blood in my ears. She looked at me again, then down at the ground. "You can't come to my house. My father doesn't like colored people. I'm sorry." Wordlessly, I handed her the bookbag and started walking the long, gray blocks home. "I'm sorry," she said again. My heart was breaking.

"I never said anything to her," I said to my therapist after telling her the story. I was all choked up. "Not one word did I say."

"Let yourself go right back to that moment. Be right there with her. Say all you have to say." I let myself see Coleen's flushed face, her small, pale hand taking the bookbag, the little gray tabby kitten in the box. As the scene shifted to the past, I lost my sense of the room, my therapist, the traffic noises outside. Everything was in the moment. Words poured out and the tears did, too. "You're hurting me. You make me feel so bad. How could you?" My rational mind understood that a child had no control of her father. But to my feelings it was all wrong. I sobbed on and on. The pain revolved around the intense feeling of being diminished, cut down, made less than a person. I was a "colored person," and that meant I couldn't go inside my friend's house. As I kept crying, the feeling spiraling deeper, I felt falsely accused of being somehow less than I was. "I'm a person, too," became my cry as I continued into the deepest part of my sorrow. I saw in my mind's eye the streets of my childhood as I made my way home.

As I arrived home in my inward journey, the feeling petered out. I lay there for a bit, then uncurled myself on the sofa and looked back at my therapist. She was still sitting quietly in the same position. I rather expected her to say something, but she stayed silent. After a few minutes I told her the story of what I'd experienced. She asked how I was feeling now. Surveying my interior, feeling landscape, I told her that, surprisingly, I still felt awful. I thought after all that crying I'd be feeling better.

"Well," she said, "it could be one of two things. Either there's more of the feeling to be felt now or this may be a feeling that, because of what you realize, leaves you sad. I suspect there may be more of the feeling. It strikes me that everything stopped as you got home. Did you tell anyone there what had happened?"

I found myself very reluctant to even think about that. The answer was no.

"Who was there?"

"Mother was, and my brothers and sisters. Daddy wasn't home from work yet."

"It seems strange that you wouldn't tell your mother."

Looking back at it, now, that did seem strange.

SILENCE

"What stopped you telling her?" my therapist asked after a few minutes of quiet.

29

"I didn't want to bother her." I could feel myself not wanting to talk about this. I wanted to forget and get out of the room.

"How could it be a bother?"

"She was always busy. She didn't like to be bothered by trivial things. I just went up to my room."

"There's that word 'trivial' again. Is this trivial?"

"No." I could feel myself squirming, wanting to escape.

"This seems to be getting hard for you to talk about. What's the matter?"

I felt so grateful to her for noticing—and for not being angry. "It really is hard. I keep wanting to escape."

"Is it some feeling with me?"

"No, it's not you. I feel really scared that something terrible is going to happen."

SILENCE

Her voice was very quiet as she said, "What you're afraid of has already happened. What is it?"

"My mother is always busy. You know that I'm the oldest of twelve children. What that means is my job is to be a help and never be a problem, unless it's a real problem. I'm not supposed to interfere with her. I can't walk up to her and say, 'I want to talk to you.' I have to wait around until she notices me."

"What happens if you don't wait?"

"She gets really angry with me."

"Do you remember a time?"

"Yes," I said, and immediately felt deeply sad.

"Tell me everything—all the details of what you remember."

"This had happened some months before the incident with Coleen."

"Let yourself talk about it just as if it is happening now," my therapist instructed me.

I followed my therapist's suggestion and started to use the present tense. I almost immediately felt smaller and more sad.

"My mother and I and several of my brothers and sisters are sitting watching something on television. It is early in the evening, but since it's wintertime, it's already pitch dark outside. We are all waiting for my father to come home. It's already six o'clock and he usually arrives exactly at five. I'm sitting to the right of Mother, not actually touching her, but close. Suddenly my younger sister, Pat, who is almost three, jumps up from her seat close to the television and runs to Mother. She flings her arms around Mother's knees and says, 'I love you, Mommy!' At that moment I feel an intense burst of love for her, too. I put one arm around Mother and one around Pat, squeezing them both, saying, 'Me, too.' Mother immediately flings me away, glaring, her eyes full of rage. Then she leans in really close to me and hisses, 'Why do you always try to steal me away from the little kids?' "

My therapist gasped and said, "She pushed you away!" Her comment confirmed my feeling. It was really as awful as it felt. I could feel the sadness welling up.

"I really wasn't trying to steal her away. I love her, too."

"Tell your mom that."

"I love you, Mommy. I really love you." I started to cry. I felt so sad. I cried harder and harder. All that love with no place to go. "She won't let me love her," I said to my therapist. "Why won't she let me love her?"

"Ask her!"

"Why won't you let me love you, too? I'm not stealing. You're my mother, too." I started crying in earnest, wailing sobs that sometimes sounded like laughter. "You hate me. You hate me. You don't love me at all. Nobody loves me." I kept on crying. Soon there was nothing to put into words, just the sound of my sadness and sorrow. Within a few minutes I was quiet again, still hurting but not knowing how to go on.

SILENCE

My therapist let the silence roll on. Finally I told her I still felt sad but didn't know what to do next.

"What happened as you were crying without words?"

"I kept seeing my mother's face glaring and hearing her voice. It hurts so much that I felt giving and she was furious with me." *Click!* The light went on. "This is just like the woman on the street. I was feeling friendly and nice and she treated me badly. And it was the same with Coleen! I was doing a good thing and again I was treated badly. I wasn't doing anything wrong." I felt immensely sad.

"Tell your mother that."

"I'm not doing anything wrong. I want to love you and you won't let me. You won't let me love you. How can you push me away? How could you? I'd never do that to you." As I said these words the sadness increased at each phrase and soon I was crying again. The pain was most intense each time I thought or said, "You won't let me love you."

"Tell her what you want," my therapist said.

"I want you to let me love you. It could be so nice. I love you so much. Please let me love you. Please. Please. I'll be good. I am good. Please let me love you. It hurts so much that I have to keep all this inside. I love you, Mother."

"You said 'Mommy' before," my therapist reminded me. It had slipped out before. Now I knew where that would lead. I shook my head. I didn't want to say that. I'd feel so naked, so exposed, so little.

"Let yourself be little," she insisted.

"I love you, Mommy," I howled with sadness. I felt so young and needy. I was a little girl again, loving my mommy with all my heart. Saying the word "Mommy" opened a hole into sadness. I'd called her "Mother" for so long. I cried and cried and cried.

"Mommy?" I questioned through my tears. The sorrow overwhelmed me. "Mommy, Mommy, Mommy, why don't you let me love you? Don't you love me? Don't you love me, Mommy?" The answer hit like a brick in the head. *No.* My mommy doesn't love me. I cried and kept on crying.

"Sometimes I feel like a motherless child. . . ." The tune and then the words of this old spiritual coursed through me, taking my sadness even deeper, because, indeed, I was a motherless child. I didn't have anyone I could go to when I was sad and hurt. It was too dangerous to approach my mother. One moment warm and understanding, the next furiously angry—I never knew how she would be. I couldn't trust her. I couldn't count on her. I had no resting place. There was no place to turn. I felt agonized, tortured, sad, but most of all, afraid. I was all alone, not alone physically, but in every other way. It was too frightening. I stopped crying. As I lay there quietly, it came to me what I'd done to survive. I could not, as a child, survive confronting how alone I was. Rather than ask for what I would not get, I stopped asking, even stopped letting myself know that I needed.

Lying still, with my eyes closed, moments, days in my life passed before my internal view. Times that I felt alone and afraid, times when I wanted to talk about things that bothered me. I never could, though. I'd learned my lesson too well. Then I thought of times when I could have spontaneously touched someone, or said something without thinking about it and calculating the response. I couldn't do that either. The risk was too great.

I began to tell my therapist all these thoughts. How terribly alone I was, so alone that I couldn't do anything that might possibly expose me to pain and rejection. I couldn't even talk to my mother about the most devastating things that had happened to me. I told my therapist how remembering "Motherless Child" had intensified the feeling.

"Would you sing it?" she asked.

I let the feeling pour into the words as I sang:

"Sometimes I feel like a motherless child
Sometimes I feel like a motherless child
Sometimes I feel like a motherless child
A long way from home, a long, long way from home."

As I sang the slow, sad dirge, I began to cry again, this time with a gentle sadness and a sympathy for myself. I didn't feel like a fool for needing my mother or other people anymore, just sad that no one had been there for me. I looked up at my therapist as I stopped crying. She reached out and gave my hand a quick little squeeze.

"That feels like my theme song, like the musical theme to a movie," I told her.

"It sounds completely appropriate," she replied, then asked, "How do you feel?"

"I feel sadness at not having been allowed to freely love my mother and at being so alone. But I feel good, a deep-down good in knowing, absolutely knowing, that I am not bad for loving and needing her."

"Do you have any other thoughts or feelings about today's session?" she asked as she turned up the lights in the semidark room.

"It's surprising to me how something as small as

that woman refusing to look at me could bring up so much pain. And it's frightening, too. Am I always going to be this sensitive? Will therapy turn me into a person who is super easily hurt?"

"Did therapy do that to you or have you been hurt like that before?"

Thinking about it, I remembered other times that I'd felt equally bad. "Well, it has happened before, but it hasn't hurt me so deeply."

"It probably did hurt you, but you defended against it more. There usually is a period in the beginning of therapy when you are more sensitive to pain, more deeply hurt than at any time since childhood. It can be a tough period, but the payoff is worth it. That payoff is more of yourself and eventually being even less vulnerable to those childhood pains, because you've felt and integrated them."

"Now that you mention it, there have been times that things like that hurt me. But instead of admitting it to myself, I'd obsess about what a creep the person was or have fantasies about getting even with them at some future time. The other thing that I'd do was to go eat a lot of cake or candy until I forgot all about it." As I told her these insights, they were a revelation to me as well.

She then asked how I was feeling about my nightmare. I told her it seemed very distant and far away.

"It seems significant to me that it popped up just after your feeling about your father. Maybe we'll talk more about it tomorrow," she said.

I left feeling surprisingly good after the misery I'd been through. I somehow felt as if I'd been on a long hike to the top of a mountain. It had been extremely hard work and I felt really tired, but satisfied and exhilarated, as well. I also knew for sure that I was on the right track. I was coming back home to myself.

Session Three

The Therapist's Voice

As my patient walked in the door, I noticed her steal a look at my face. She seemed nervous and twitchy, and took a long time settling, but finally she was lying on the thickly carpeted floor with her head resting on a pillow. I sat behind her in the dimly lit room, quietly waiting for her to begin. As is usually the case with patients during this intensive period, I'd been thinking about her off and on since the day before, but especially on my way to the office. My drive through rush-hour traffic had been punctuated by questions of how she'd been feeling and what would be happening today.

She gave a deep, long sigh. After a pause I remarked, "That was a deep sigh; what's happening inside?"

Another pause and deep sigh. She hesitated, then began to speak. "I've been thinking so much about my childhood. I've always thought that it was a bad one, but now I'm beginning to see just how bad."

"Hmm, would you like to talk about it?" Not wanting her to focus on me rather than herself, I purposely didn't say, "Tell me."

"My father didn't like me," she said, with a little catch in her voice.

My heart gave a little dip. I could feel how sad she was. Rather than take her away from her feeling by using a conversational tone or a rationalizing discussion about why her father behaved as he did, I chose to increase the intensity of what she felt.

"He didn't like his own daughter?"

"No, I don't think he did," she said. "He was never happy to see me, and he never helped me when I needed him to."

She had suddenly become restless again, twisting and turning as she lay there on the carpet. I could see she was struggling with something.

"You sounded so sad when you said he didn't like you."

"I am sad, and I want to cry, but it feels stuck in my throat."

"What does it feel like inside when you want to cry this way?"

"Everything feels heavy and dark, my stomach and chest are tight, and it's the most tight around my throat."

"Let yourself give another deep sigh and see what it feels like when you say he doesn't like you." Again I wanted to help deepen the feeling.

"My father doesn't like me. My father doesn't like me."

"Is that what you called him when you were little?"

"No, we all called him 'Daddy.' "

"Call him that now." Using this childhood language would help her stay in touch with the child feeling rather than remain the adult just talking about her childhood.

"My daddy doesn't like me." She put her hands over her face and started to cry quietly. "I can't believe he doesn't like me. I can't believe it." She cried some more, then stopped.

She was quiet for a while; then I asked, "What is it?"

"I don't want to think about it. I don't want to remember what it was like every day." A few more tears trickled down her face.

"It's very hard, isn't it?" I said, letting my sympathy show in my voice. "But you can't really forget, can you? Let yourself see what it was like every day."

"We were always afraid. I never remember feeling easy with him or having a quiet conversation. There was always tension and fear, the need to watch his moods very carefully, to keep from setting him off. When he wasn't there I remember us kids playing, running, and jumping about. My mother was much easier to be around. She could lose her temper quickly, too, but she wasn't violent the way he was. It was funny the way I felt about him. Even though I was so afraid, and I clearly remember hating him at times, I very much loved him. I thought he was wonderful looking and I even felt proud of him being my daddy. He came home every day at five o'clock, on the dot. My mother would bathe and dress us just before, so we would be clean and nice when he arrived. We'd watch really closely down the street to see him coming. Then we'd wave to him, flailing our arms back and forth. He'd give one little flick with his newspaper. When he got to the front porch, he'd give each one of us one pat on the top of our heads, one through six, then stride into the house. No smiles and no kisses. He didn't like me. He didn't like any of us."

At this last she began to cry in earnest. "Daddy doesn't like any of us. Our daddy doesn't like us." She cried softly into the pillow, hiding her face.

Again, I, too, felt some sadness, thinking of what she'd suffered and knowing there was more to come. I sat back and listened. I could tell from the tone of her cry that she was very sad but she was also holding back, purposely being as quiet as possible. Then I said, "Let it out. It's all right to cry. Let it all come out."

She did open up a little more and cried more freely for about ten minutes, then dribbled to a stop. She felt around for the tissue box, which I passed to her. After wiping her face and blowing her nose she said, "I can't believe that he didn't like us."

SILENCE

In that silence, I wondered if she was ready to

confront her father in the feeling or if she needed to "set the scene" a bit more. I decided to see; rather than ask her a question that would elicit more details of the past, I directed her into the feeling. If this didn't help, I could always come back and ask questions later. "Tell him that."

SILENCE

"I can't believe you don't like us. I can't believe it. Why did you have us? Why did you have us if you just want to hurt us? All you do is hurt us." She burst into sobs, crying deep and hard. "You hurt us. You hurt us. You hurt us." She turned over on her stomach and curled around the pillow.

I sat back in my seat and let her go. There was nothing for me to do now but wait until she needed to talk to me again. I knew from the autobiography that she'd written to apply to the Institute that she'd been beaten a lot as a child. I wasn't sure if that was what her feeling was about; it wasn't important, for now, that I know. The important thing was that *she* know. I could always find out later. As she cried on I saw an image of a little girl afraid of her father, physically afraid, a little girl who had a mother she was afraid to talk to. I knew she had a hard road to follow in therapy. I wondered if this was the end point of what she would need to feel this day or whether this was just the beginning. She cried steadily for fifteen minutes, then fell silent. I respected that silence, knowing that in these silent spaces after deep feeling, memories and clear insight might well emerge.

"I always feel so sorry for the little kids. They are too little to understand what's happening."

These were her first words after crying. I knew by her use of the present tense that she was still very close to her childhood pain. I thought to myself, You felt sorry for the "little kids"? But you were still so small yourself. What I said was, "How old were you?"

"Eleven."

"That doesn't sound very big to me."

SILENCE

"I wasn't, really. I always felt so big, though; the younger ones would all come to me after he hurt us."

"And who would you go to?"

SILENCE

"There was no one," was eventually her reply.

"So you were alone."

"Yes, I really was."

"You cried very hard when you were saying 'You hurt us.' How did he hurt you?"

There was a silence and then, shamefaced, she replied, "He beat us." She quickly changed this, then saying, "He spanked us."

"What's the difference?" I asked.

"Spanking is when he hits us with his hand a few times and beating is when he hits us with a belt or something a lot of times."

I tagged that "or something" with a red flag in my mind for later. For now, I simply said sympathetically, "It sounds as if you know the difference from experience."

"I do."

"Were you mostly spanked or beaten?"

She looked to the side, then slowly said, "Beaten."

"Oh. You changed it to 'spanked' when you first talked about it."

SILENCE

"I don't like to talk about it."

"How do you feel when you do talk about it?"

"I feel ashamed. I feel dirty and bad."

"*You* feel ashamed! Ashamed of what?"

"Even though I know he shouldn't have beaten us, it feels as if it proves we were bad."

"Were you that bad? That you should be beaten with a belt 'or something'?"

"I don't think we were."

"What specific event were you feeling about when you cried earlier?"

SILENCE

"I hate to talk about this. It makes me hate myself."

"When you feel it through, I don't think you'll be hating yourself. Please try to talk about it."

Slowly at first, then with gathering speed, she began: "When I was eleven years old we lived near a library, and my parents gave me permission to go there one Saturday. My younger sister, who was six, came along with me. She sneaked out and was playing on the escalator to the subway when she was caught by one of our neighbors and taken home. I discovered she was gone and ran home to tell my parents she was lost. When I got there my mother was sitting in the living room talking quietly with the neighbor and my father was in the kitchen with my sister. My mother sent me in with them. He was questioning her about what she'd done. He was furious and he kept saying, 'Didn't we tell you to stay with your sister? Didn't we tell you that? You just don't know how to do what you're told, do you?'

" 'Daddy, I promise I'll never do it again. Daddy, Daddy, I promise,' my sister was pleading, and she was shaking and crying.

" 'Crying won't help you now,' he said with a sneery smile on his face. 'You should have thought of that before.'

" 'She won't do it again, Daddy,' I quavered. I was scared to say anything more. He whirled toward me. 'And *you*—I'm about two seconds off you. Get upstairs and I'll deal with you later. Get out of here.'

"He didn't have to tell me twice. I ran from the room and went upstairs. Then I went immediately to the heating duct that led from the kitchen to my brothers' bedroom. They were already there, along with another sister. I was just in time to hear my father say, 'You're coming with me, young lady, while I teach you a lesson you'll never forget.' I heard the basement door slam and my sister's pleading. We all looked at one another in horror and fear. I knew I was next. We ran to the bathroom, which had a heating duct that led from the basement. We could hear everything. We could hear her pleading and begging; we could hear him talking in a gloating voice.

Sometimes he almost laughed. We could hear the whistling sound of the blows falling. She started screaming and then we could hear him ordering her to be quiet. She tried but still the strangled moans and sobs carried clearly through the ducts. We were crying, too, but silently, so he wouldn't hear us."

I listened in outrage and sadness. This was what the child she was had suffered. All through the narrative tears had been running down her face. At the end she began to cry silently.

"Don't keep it in! It's safe to let it out here!" I told her.

"I'm sorry. I'm sorry. I'm sorry. I can't do anything to help you. I tried. I can't help you. Please forgive me. I'm sorry I didn't watch you closer so you didn't go outside. I'm sorry. I'm so sorry. I can't stand it."

Now she was shouting and sobbing and rolling on the floor in her agony. She cried and she cried and she cried. She started talking to God. "Dear God, please don't let him kill her. Please somebody help her. I can't help. I'll be good forever if only you'll help her." She cried a high, keening cry, then dropped into deep, low sobs. She suddenly got quieter, but she was clenching and unclenching her fists.

"Let it out!" I instructed her again.

"I hate myself. I hate myself. I hate myself. If only I'd watched her better, she wouldn't be getting hurt now. It's all my fault. I'm a coward. I should have done something to make him stop."

"Like what?"

"Told him to stop."

"Do it *now.*"

"Stop! Stop! Stop hitting her. You're hurting her. You're killing her. You just hurt everyone. Stop. Stop. Stop!" She shouted and she shrieked. The last "stop" went on for several seconds.

I was leaning forward, watching very closely. I was horrified and satisfied at the same time—horrified at what she'd witnessed and experienced, satisfied that finally she was getting release.

"Stop hitting her. Stop it. Listen to me, Daddy. She's only a little girl. How can you hurt her so much? She loves you. How can you hurt her this much? Why are you doing this to her? Why? Why? Why? Why? Tell me, why? Is it because she's not good? But we all try so hard to be good. We clean the house. We're good at school. We're always polite. We don't lie. We don't steal. We do everything we can think of. But you are never happy with any of us. You never kiss us. You never hug us. You just scare us and beat us. You like doing it. You like it. You like hurting us. Don't you love us even a little tiny bit? Just the tiniest bit? No, I don't think you do. You smile more at the dog." Here she broke down even more, crying and sobbing with all her might. She kept crying, now without words but still very deeply. After some time, she abruptly stopped. I was still watching her every expression. She didn't have the peaceful, relaxed look of someone finished with her feeling. Instead, she looked outraged.

"Say what you're feeling," I interjected. I didn't

want to ask her questions, which I knew could distract her from her feeling.

"I'm not the one who should be sorry," she said fiercely. "*He* should be sorry."

"Tell him."

"*You*, you, you're the bad one. You should be sorry, but you're not. You're never sorry. *We* always have to be sorry. You made her bleed. She couldn't go to school. She couldn't walk. Because of you. That's not love. You are not a father! I didn't do anything bad. I don't hate myself. I *won't* hate myself. I hate you! I hate you!" She was still crying, but this time it was a cry of rage. She kept clenching her fists.

"It's okay. Do what you feel."

She began pounding on the pillow as she said again and again, "I hate you. We all hate you. You tell us you beat us because we're so bad. We are not bad! *You* are bad. *You* are mean. I don't want you for my daddy. I want a real daddy who loves me. I want a real daddy!" This last phrase she repeated over and over and over. Her cries eventually grew softer and softer; then very quietly she said, "I'll never be like you and I'll never forget."

She turned over on her back, her eyes closed, her face to the ceiling; there was a serenity and even a relaxed beauty that I'd never seen there before. It was a child's face—totally open, with nothing to control or hide. She lay there quietly for a good five minutes, then looked back and said with a hint of a smile, "I guess I had a primal."

"I guess you did."

"I can never believe that I'll feel good again if I start to cry, but somehow I always do."

"Most often, if you are able to finish the feeling you do feel good afterward. But sometimes there's some sadness left or sometimes the feeling is too intense to finish at one go." I wanted her to know the reality, not to view this process as some magic trick.

"I understand. This was a very hard feeling for me to go into. After I'd started to cry at the very beginning I could see where it was going, and as much as I came to therapy to feel, something in me didn't want to go there."

"Understandably so, because it is so painful."

"I want to tell you the rest of the story, but I don't think I can feel any more of it today."

"Fine."

"He beat my sister so much that when she came upstairs she had bloody welts all over her thighs and buttocks and her hands were all bruised and swollen, too, because she'd tried to protect herself. She got into bed and fell asleep. My mother found her later. I know my mother was angry with my father and they had a huge fight that night, but my sister wasn't taken to a doctor. She just stayed home in bed for about a week and then went back to school. My mother told me later that she was afraid my father would go to jail and there would be no one to support us."

"Was that the truth?"

"I don't think so because years later when she went

to work and made as much or more money than he did, she still stayed. And he kept beating us like that."

"And she let him do that? She didn't try to protect you?"

"Sometimes she did, but then he would turn on her and hit her."

"Sounds like no one had it easy in your family, except maybe your father."

"He never got hit, that's for sure. We were all afraid of him."

"Do you see effects in your present life from these feelings?"

"Yes. First, I don't trust men. I always think and feel that they can all suddenly get violent. That's the way it was with Daddy; he could get furious and start hitting us in a split second. You never knew when it could come. We were always afraid of him, but trying to please him at the same time. I remember loving him very much when I was little and wanting to be so good so he would love me, too. But he never did. I started dating late, and it's not easy for me in relationships now. I want and need to be loved and liked so much that I try hard to do everything perfectly because the consequences were so terrible when anything went wrong. So if a man seems to like me even a little bit I'm practically willing to be his slave."

"It sounds as if you're stuck between a rock and a hard place. On one side is fear and on the other side need."

"Exactly. That's the way it was with Daddy, too.

Only he never even pretended to give what I need. Then there's that feeling of hating myself and feeling bad because I couldn't save my sister. It got so clear in the feeling, though. If I had had a real father, I wouldn't have to try to do more than a child could do. He's the one who was meant to protect us, not the one we needed protection *from.* I always felt wrong and bad and ashamed of myself. But he's the one who should feel ashamed. Since I've grown up I have often *thought* that he was the wrong one but I always *felt* that I was wrong. There's a big difference."

"What's the difference for you?" I wanted to be sure she had the intellectual understanding as well as the feeling connection. I knew articulating her thoughts would help her understanding.

"When I just think it, I still have a lurking feeling that something's wrong with me. When I felt it today, every tiny bit of me felt a wrong had been done to me and my little sister, not that I had done something wrong. On some level I always blamed myself. But I am not to blame. I wonder, though, if that blaming myself feeling will come back."

"It could, because there is so much pain and so many levels of the feeling that it probably will come up again and again. One deep feeling doesn't wipe out all traces of sorrow that deep. There are many levels of pain in this one incident. I suspect that you've been taught to blame yourself in many other areas of your life as well, so it will probably come up elsewhere. You can't undo a lifetime of pain in one sitting. Fortunately, you have the possibility of recognizing it as an old feeling now, at least some of the time, and of tracing it back and feeling it in the past where it started."

"That makes sense."

"Can you tell me what happened in your feeling? Of course I could see and hear you as you felt, but I don't know what you experienced from the inside."

"One surprising thing for me was I didn't care how I sounded or looked. I usually worry that I look or sound stupid. The biggest surprise was that I went back. It was like a time machine or at least what I imagine of one from reading science fiction. I was *there*. I could smell the kitchen smells; the dusty smell of the heating duct; the sounds; what everyone was wearing, facial expressions—*everything* came back. When I was shouting to my father to stop I could see the little squares of the grillwork on the heating duct. I felt as if I were shouting down through all the years. I didn't know I could feel that angry. If intensity of feeling could kill, my father would have died of a heart attack during this session."

"We've never lost one that way yet," I told her. I was also thinking that from her description, she had experienced the feeling on a very deep level, a resolving level. Her thoughts and insights were very lucid, without the confusion that can arise when the patient hasn't been able to go deep enough in the pain to reach resolution.

"How did you know I was angry and needed to tell him?"

"I was watching what your body was doing. You repeatedly clenched and unclenched your hands into fists. That can be a clue for you when you are feeling on your own. Your body can be trusted, and it knows where your feeling needs to go long before your mind catches on."

"It really helped that you encouraged me right then; I could feel myself getting angry but I didn't quite know what to do or if it was okay to be angry."

"Whatever you feel is okay here. Trust your feelings, because they are trustworthy. Also, do tell me the things that are helpful to you as well as the ones that interfere or don't help. That will help me to help you better. Everyone is different and things that aid one person are often a hindrance for another."

"Okay, I'll try to tell you when I notice something," she replied.

"I just thought of something that I meant to ask you. Did your father beat you that day?"

"I was thinking about that before and forgot it in telling you something else. He didn't beat me that day, which gave me another thing to feel bad about. I was so very relieved, but at the same time I felt guilty, since my sister was beaten and I wasn't. I think what happened is that he got scared at how much and how violently he beat her. He never said anything to me about it, but I lived in terror for days that he was going to beat me at any moment."

"That must have been torture."

"It was. I remember skulking around the house, trying to keep out of his sight."

More feelings she doesn't even know are there, I thought to myself, but we'd save them for another day. "Is there anything more you'd like us to talk about?" I knew she had to be tired. We'd been in session for two and a half hours.

"No, I think I'm all talked and felt out."

"Okay, I'll see you in the afternoon tomorrow in case you can use a little extra sleep time. Call if you need me and take it easy. You've done a lot of feeling."

"What do mean by 'take it easy'?"

"I mean for you to do whatever feels nurturing and comforting to you. For you that might mean taking a walk in the park, or having a bubble bath, or having sweet, beautiful flowers in your room. Do something kind for yourself. It's very important to make sure you have good things in your present life as you work on deep feelings. If you are just as deprived now as you were in your childhood, it can become impossible to let yourself go there in your feelings. You need to sleep, eat well, and have some fun in the present, in order to feel the past pain."

"You mean if I deny myself good things, it will make therapy harder?"

"Yes, that is exactly what I mean."

"Okay, that's good to know. See you tomorrow."

With a jaunty wave of her hand she set out, back into the outside world. As I returned to my office, I thought how sad it was that she'd suffered so. I suddenly recalled Shakespeare's King Lear, another father who couldn't see real love when it was there for the taking and who didn't know how to love his child. I shook my head and went into my office.

Session Four

The Therapist's Voice

NOT SURPRISINGLY, AFTER SUCH AN INTENSE SESsion, my patient stayed on my mind. As the day passed I wondered how she was faring and whether more of the same feeling was coming up. Puttering around the house that night, I kept thinking of her. I especially was curious about how she would be at her next session. I'd worked with many people who got frightened by such intensity of feeling and then shut down completely for a day or so; other patients would do the same from exhaustion. I reminded myself that if she had been frightened by today's session, we'd take it a bit more slowly tomorrow.

The next morning she was on my mind again as I threaded my way through the rush-hour traffic. I really didn't know what to expect. Over the years I'd seen every reaction, from total resistance the next day to the patient bursting into tears without a word being said. I'd have to just wait and see.

When she came in she seemed quiet but she did make eye contact. I thought to myself, Good, a bit of trust is building. As usual, I just waited to let her start wherever she wanted. After a while she quietly said, "I've been thinking about my father a lot since yesterday. It was even scary thinking about him. I let myself get so angry yesterday that it almost seemed there had to be some retribution. At home I really got into trouble if any expression of anger crept out. He seemed to know if I was even *thinking* anything angry.

"In a way, it surprised me that I was able to get so angry yesterday. I've never talked back to him in real life. I've always been too afraid."

"Your comment interests me because I did wonder during the session yesterday if you would be able to let that anger out. It was very clear that you felt angry, but letting it out is sometimes hard to do when you've been frightened so much. What allowed you to express it so freely?"

"It was a combination of things. First, you let me know it was okay to feel as I do. Secondly, the feeling was so intense that it really wanted to come out; once it got started it seemed to have a life of its own. The other thing that feels very important is that I remember feeling during my childhood that he was wrong, that he shouldn't be treating us this way—all mixed in with blaming myself and feeling ashamed."

"What gave you that sense about him?"

"Some of our relatives were very nice to us, and for the same things that Daddy would give us a beating, such as spilling something or getting rowdy as we were playing, they would accept an apology instead of getting furiously angry. That gave me the feeling that he was doing something wrong. If everybody had been mean I don't think I could have said those things to him yesterday. The other thing was how he acted when we were hurt. He never behaved like the fathers on television did when their children got hurt. He was never like my uncles or my grandmother. If I got hurt when I was with them, they tried to help me, like Mother did when I stepped on the nail. I just feel like I never had a real father."

SILENCE

"What makes a real father?" I knew, by her continued use of the phrase "real father," that she had a strong sense of what she needed in a father. I was certain that her answer to this question would lead to pain.

"A real father is someone you can count on. A real father loves you and is kind to you. And a real father helps you when you need help. I can remember time after time after time when he didn't help me, when he even hurt me."

"How does it make you feel—that you never had any of those 'real father' things?"

"It makes me feel so sad when I think of all those times he wasn't there when I needed him."

I could feel her sadness permeate the room. "Are there particular incidents you remember?"

"There was the time I was chased over and over again by two bullies in my neighborhood. When I asked Daddy for help, he just said in a voice full of contempt, 'Can't you handle that yourself? Well, you'll have to.' There was also the time he took me to the dentist and I started to cry and squirm while the dentist drilled my tooth without anesthetic. The dentist called my father in out of the waiting room. Instead of telling him to give me an anesthetic or talking to me nicely, Daddy threatened to beat me right there in the dentist's office if I didn't shut up. He stood there and glared at me until the dentist finished. The dental pain was easier to bear than running the risk of him beating me. You already know about the time I stepped on the nail."

Momentarily overwhelmed by the images of her standing alone against the bullies, then being virtually tortured in the dentist's office, I gasped. "How could he do that?" burst from my lips.

"He just doesn't care about me," she sadly said.

I was stymied here. Which direction should we go? I didn't know which of the incidents she'd remembered was more important, and the moments were ticking by. Then I had it. I wasn't the one to decide where to go—she was. "Do the bullies or the dentist bring that feeling the most?" I asked.

"The dentist, because how could Daddy stand there and watch? I was in agony, and I know it showed on my face. There wasn't one moment of kindness or compassion. He just stood there like a block of wood and let the dentist grind into my tooth." She fell silent.

I could feel my heart rate speed up. Now what to do? I could feel how close she was to opening up, and I didn't want to waste any words or time helping her into the feeling. But I also knew the danger of going too fast. Pushing her into a feeling before she was ready could easily lead to her shutting down or getting too frightened to feel. Going too slowly was also a danger because she could miss the opening, the place where she had an open doorway to the feeling. Everything depended on the proper timing. Telling her to talk to her father, to say her feeling, would definitely be premature here.

"Let yourself tell the whole story," I said. This would keep us on the line of pain without being too intense and probing.

"I was six years old and this was my first trip to the dentist. I don't know why Mommy didn't take me since she usually took us to the doctor. But I had my first cavity and it needed to be filled. I was called in from the waiting room; my father stayed there.

"The dentist had me sit in the chair and he tilted it back. He told me to open my mouth really widely, and then he took the drill and started in on one of my back teeth. Almost immediately I was in so much pain I didn't know what to do. I started to move and he ordered me to be still because he could hurt me more by drilling my tongue or cheek. I tried, but I could not be still. I started crying and then he angrily stopped drilling and went to the door. He called my father in and said something about how Daddy had to control me because he couldn't. Daddy gave me a look. One of those that we kids called 'the Look.' It meant he was just about to hit us if we didn't stop whatever it was we were doing. Next he said, 'I don't want to beat you right here, but I will if I have to.' Then he told the dentist to go ahead. He stood about a foot behind the dentist and just stared and glared at me. Each time I would begin to groan or squirm he would narrow his eyes and just that small gesture would make me stop. I was in great pain but I was more afraid of a beating from him than the agony of my tooth."

SILENCE

I was stunned. There were so many feelings in her story that I didn't know which way to direct her. I myself was a bundle of feelings from listening. The silence wore on. I wanted to say something but I wasn't sure what. Finally I said, "I'm stunned. How could he let that happen to you?"

"I don't know."

All through the telling of this story, she had been very low-key but obviously extremely sad. There hadn't been any one moment that was more relevant than another. They were all loaded. I decided to go with that and let her direct the feeling.

"Let's go back into those moments. Let yourself be sitting right there in the dentist's chair. Be right there and tell me all the little details you see and remember." If it worked, this technique could help connect her to the specific feeling of the moment, rather than just the general sadness.

SILENCE

I let the silence roll on. I could see my patient slipping deeper into her memories of that time. Her expression was one of extreme concentration; her eyes were closed. Suddenly she opened them.

"I remember the smells. I hate that smell. That burning smell of my tooth being drilled. I hate it. The smell and the look in my father's eyes. They make me feel sick." I could feel the tension building. I knew she would break down into the feeling at any moment.

"Stay right there. Be that little girl."

"I'm scared. I'm scared of the dentist. I'm scared of the pain. But most of all I'm scared of Daddy."

"Tell him."

"I'm scared of you. I'm scared. I'm so scared."

She began to cry with a vengeance. Tears poured down her face. She sobbed and cried. "Why do I have to be so afraid of you? I shouldn't be so afraid of you. But I am, I'm more afraid of you than anything. You scare me. I'm all alone. I'm all alone. There's no place I can turn. I just have to sit here and be hurt with you looking on. You are not a real daddy. A real daddy wouldn't let this happen to his child. I want a real daddy. I want a real daddy. I want my real daddy. If I'm good, will you be a real daddy? I'll be so good. Please. I promise."

She was curled in a tight ball, on her side, clutching a pillow to her chest and stomach. She was crying with gut-wrenching force, not stopping for a second. I could see her stomach heaving up and down. She bounced from crying about wanting a real daddy to feeling all alone. The deepest sobs overtook her as she cried about the aloneness. There was even a lonely sound to her cry. "I shouldn't be so alone with this pain. I'm too little. I'm too little. It hurts too much. It hurts too much. I can't. I can't. I can't. I need somebody. I need somebody to be here, and there isn't anybody. There's nobody. There's nobody. Even if I'm good, nobody is here."

She kept on and on. Each time she cycled around to the aloneness her cries were so desperately desolate, inconsolable. At the same time, she was not dramatic. Sometimes she cried softly, sometimes more loudly, but each time it came from the heart of her pain. As I sat there tears came into the corners of my eyes. I agreed with her. At six she had been too little to see and know that she was all alone, that there was no father to protect her and care for her needs. She hadn't been able to bear that knowledge then and I could clearly see why. I found myself having fantasies of jumping into her feeling and slapping her father in the face, telling him what an abomination he was. If it brought up that much anger in me and it wasn't even my story, what a volcano of rage had to be seething inside her. I was sure that would be for another day.

Slowly her feeling began to wind down, with little starts and stutters of more feeling. At one point she burst out with, "I'm so tired. But there's no place to rest. There is no resting place for me." She carried on crying with deep, sorrowful sobs. Then she came out with "I don't have a daddy. I only have a father. I don't have a daddy. I don't even have a daddy."

When she said the word "even" she broke all the way down again. That word meant something very deep in the throes of her feeling. She cried with deep, long sobs. She sounded so young. "I don't even have a daddy," she cried out again. "I want a daddy," she wailed, "I want one so much. Why can't I have one like everybody else?" Again she cried and cried.

There was nothing for me to do but be a presence in the room with her pain. Slowly, her crying died out until the room was silent. The silence went on for a long time. I could feel that this had been a natural stopping place for her feeling, and I had no intention of interrupting her rhythm of coming out of the depths. Her breathing slowed and she continued to lie there quietly. After about ten minutes she gave a stretch and reached for the box of tissues. She gave a long, loud honk of her nose, then looked up at me and said, "That's what a real father is, a resting place. The person you go to when things get to be too much, when they hurt too much, or they're too scary. I've never had that with my father. I never had a real father at all."

"No, it looks as if you never did."

Both of us were speaking slowly and softly, in marked contrast to our voices leading up to the feeling and when she was in it. I always noticed that in a "good" session, the pace changed completely by the end of the feeling. I knew this was because instead of trying to run away from what she had been feeling inside, she had confronted and felt it, leaving her with nothing she needed to defend against. She was in a state of peace. She seemed fragile and extremely open. She fell silent again, and I waited for her to initiate our talking together. Oftentimes major insights take place during these silent moments after a deep feeling. But this was her ball game and it was up to her to throw the ball. She was breathing slowly and evenly, staring into nothingness.

"I was so afraid of my father. I can never explain to anyone how frightening he was. I walked around with a pit of fear in my stomach every day. I really feared for my life. When I would try to talk about it to anyone before I came here I couldn't really do it, because I usually get afraid just talking about him. Here it's okay because I can cry when I get the scared feeling. Everything begins to shake inside me when I really let myself think about some of the things he did to me and to my brothers and sisters. Since I left home I usually try not to think about him at all. When he's been on my mind a lot in the past it's affected the way I do things. I'm much more frightened to take risks of any kind when I'm close to feelings about him, because risks bring up the feeling of danger—the danger that I lived with every day from him. I just learned to take up as little room as possible and to keep out of his sight."

"You suffered a lot." Here I wanted to be sure to confirm her reality. Often a patient who has suffered as she did will find it difficult to truly acknowledge the pain and will try to diminish and belittle his or her suffering.

SILENCE

"Actually I did. But I find it very hard to simply admit that. Everything in me wants to protest and say I didn't have it so bad. But it was bad, that is the truth."

"I noticed in your feeling that you bounced back and forth between two things, the fear and the aloneness." I knew that articulating what she understood at this moment could help solidify her insight and realization.

"It was like a knife with a point at each end. When I couldn't take the pain anymore with one thing, it would jump to the other. Both were too much. The aloneness is almost worse than the fear. That aloneness is like my worst nightmare. Wow! It's like the nightmare that I told you, the one with the giant wolves. I'm terrified *and* I'm completely alone with nowhere to turn."

"Was that a recurring nightmare?"

"No. Well, actually I guess it is. I had it that one time I can remember. That was enough. After that dream I didn't remember my dreams for years, but then I had it again the other night."

"I guess your dreams could clearly see the reality of your life."

"Yes, the reality that I had nowhere to turn and my father was the person I most needed to run from."

"What makes you see that?"

"The only person that inspires that fear, that terror, is my father. In the dream he turned up as a man-eating wolf. But in real life my father was just that frightening."

"Whew! No wonder you fear risky things now. Was there ever any relief?" I asked this question to get a clearer picture of what had helped her survive as well as she had.

"The greatest relief was my maternal great-grandmother and that whole side of my family. My other escape was reading."

"What about your mother?"

"Sometimes she was a help, but many times she only made things worse. I remember one time when I was trying to be especially good by cleaning the house to perfection. My mother got furiously angry and accused me of trying to make her look bad. What could I do with that?"

"Trying to make her look bad?"

"My father complimented me and she got angry. That was another time she misjudged me. She often thought the worst of me, when I had done my best to be really good. There was no one to turn to for relief."

Again I was stunned. Everything I thought of to say in reply felt trivial. All I could do was give a "humph" of amazement.

"It's hard to believe, isn't it? When I really think

about how I grew up it surprises me that I'm not a junkie or a criminal."

"What was the saving grace?" I knew there had to be one or she would have been in much worse shape in her daily life. I wanted *her* to be as aware as possible of what helped her, as well as the events that caused her pain. In addition, I didn't want her to think that only her pain was important in the course of therapy.

"I'm sure it was the love of MaMa—my great-grandmother—and some of my older relatives. They provided a contrast of some kindness to all that meanness. Without that, I don't know. I just don't know."

SILENCE

"Without her, I think I would have turned out to be a much meaner person. If there's no kindness, no goodness around you, the only protection is to be mean yourself. She was the example of the other way of being."

"What was she like?"

"She looked like the typical grandmother, with white hair in a bun. She wore long dresses and worked a lot in her garden. That was a really good time to talk to her. She would be weeding or planting and I would be working right beside her. We would do a little digging and then a little talking. She had a strong moral sense and was very religious. When I think about her now, though, the things she taught me weren't based very much on organized religion. It all had to do with kindness. She really believed in being kind, but not in a wimpy way. She was very able to stand up for what was right. My father didn't beat us when we were at her house. I remember her telling him 'that's enough' when he was working himself up to hitting us. He would leave us alone then. She taught me the Golden Rule: 'Do unto others as you would have them do unto you.' That lesson of hers really helped me later in life. My father often beat me when my younger brothers and sisters would do something wrong. He would say it was my responsibility what they did. I would get really angry with them and want to beat them, and sometimes did. But by remembering my great-grandmother I would many times not hit them. I would think that I didn't want to be as mean as he was and that I wanted to be a kind person like her. Other times I was just a typical short-tempered abused person taking it out on someone else."

"How would you take it out on them?"

"When my parents went out, starting when I was about ten years old, I would be completely in charge. I had permission to beat the other kids just as my parents did or to punish them as I saw fit. And if they did something wrong while my parents were gone and my parents found out about it, I would be beaten. The temptation to pay them back for getting me into trouble was really strong. Or sometimes it was the fear. I was terrified of what my father would do to me and I would terrify them into behaving. I would scream and yell and shout and hit them to make them do the things Daddy wanted, like cleaning the house or washing the clothes. That's what I feel bad about. That I would be like him. My consolation was that most of the time I wasn't like him and that I did protect them from him at times by lying or taking the blame for things myself. And I did apologize when I was unjust."

"Those were very trying times."

"They were. I so much don't want to be like my father. I worked really hard at controlling my temper. I usually feel really bad when I get angry because it seems I'm turning into him. It's funny, though; I didn't feel like a bad person after my rage with him yesterday. I just felt afraid I would get into trouble. I wonder why that is?"

"What do you think?"

"I think he deserved for me to be angry with him. And my brothers and sisters didn't deserve it. I was taking it out on them. This time in my feeling the anger went where it belonged. . . . You know, like in those police movies, my father was the perpetrator, the one who committed the crime."

"In your feeling today it seems that the feeling was more concentrated around the sadness."

"Yes, I really was. I felt little flashes of anger, but the deepest feeling for me was the aloneness and the sadness of not having a father."

"It seemed to hurt you very deeply when you said, 'I don't even have a daddy.' Each time you said 'even' you cried so desolately."

"It hurt so much that I didn't have a daddy like other children do. Every time I said 'even' it felt that a bottomless hole of emptiness and sadness opened up. I can't describe in words how painful it is."

"Some feelings can't be fully expressed in words. That's why we have to cry. How are you feeling now?"

"I feel okay. There's a touch of sadness, but it feels real. I'm not pretending to myself that it doesn't matter that I don't have a daddy. It does matter; it makes me sad at what I missed. I think I'm pretty well cried out for today. I'm glad I talked about my great-grandmother. I've always known how much I love her, but I never thought before how she saved me from being more like my father."

As she spoke she was gathering up her things, throwing the used tissues in the trash, putting on her shoes. When she finished she looked me straight in the eye, paused a moment, then said, "Thank you."

"You are welcome," was my reply.

Session Five

The Patient Speaks

I LEFT THE SESSION WITH A TRACE OF LINGER-
ing sadness, which felt appropriate. I was sad that I
didn't have a real father. The nature of the sadness I
was used to carrying around had changed, however;
now it seemed a peaceful sadness, not desperate or
miserable. I thought a lot about MaMa, my great-
grandmother; small things about her kept flashing
through my mind. I reminded myself that I wanted
to talk more about her in my next session.

The world I saw walking down the street was far removed from my childhood; the flamboyant people
and the expensive cars of Los Angeles really seemed
from another world. Everywhere I looked I saw another beautiful person or boutique. The dichotomy
was too intense. Quickening my pace, I headed back

to my motel and the quiet of my memories. I entered the world of my journal, noting the feelings I had experienced in the session. I suddenly felt exhausted and wanted only to sleep. I was struck by how much energy having a feeling used. Now it was clear why I wasn't allowed to work or go to school during the intensive. There just wouldn't be enough energy to go around. I got back to the room and snuggled down in bed in the middle of the day—a luxury I normally never allowed myself. When I woke from my nap I felt good and wanted something to eat. I went to one of the coffee shops in the area, had a quick hamburger, and, thinking of what my therapist had said about "being nice" to myself, I also indulged in a piece of devil's food chocolate cake! It was wonderful. Then I went back to the room. I was feeling lonely. I wished it was okay to call someone—my boyfriend, maybe, or one of my sisters. I wasn't used to having nothing to do, or to being so alone. Not being allowed to read was especially hard for me. I walked and paced around the room. I wasn't at all sleepy, but with nothing else to do I got ready for bed. I kept thinking about MaMa and again reminded myself that I wanted to tell my therapist more about her the next day. I finally fell asleep, still thinking about the next day's session.

When I woke in the morning I was still feeling pretty good, though I did keep checking to see if I could discover a feeling. I suddenly noticed how much I *wanted* to have a feeling to tell my therapist about so I could be a good patient. "How sick," I thought. Then

I reminded myself that that was why I had come to therapy, to stop being driven by the "shoulds" and "musts." If I didn't do that anymore I'd be cured. I wondered if I really would be all better at the end of the three-week intensive. It seemed impossible, but I desperately hoped so. I was tired of feeling the way I did most of the time—so frightened or worried about what people were thinking of me. I wanted some kind of peace.

As I arrived for my session, my therapist met me at the door as she usually did, with a quiet "Good morning." It really didn't seem so difficult to look her in the eye these days, though I did get a few small butterflies in my stomach at the beginning of each session.

"It's getting a bit easier being here every day," I started out by saying.

"How so?" she queried.

"The first few days I was so afraid to look you in the eye. I don't know exactly what I was afraid of. . . ."

SILENCE

"No idea?"

"Actually, yes I do. I was afraid I'd see a look in your eyes that said you didn't want to be here or you didn't like me."

SILENCE

"And if you had?"

"Then it would have been terrible, because I need your help, and if I had seen that look, I couldn't get it."

"Why not?"

"Well, if someone doesn't really want to help you,

even if they do the thing that has to be done, you still don't get help."

"What do you mean?"

"If someone helps you begrudgingly, you're left with the pain."

"What pain?"

"It comes back to the pain of not being cared about."

"So, what would you have done if you had seen that 'not caring' look in my eyes those first few days?"

Whoops! Now I was in trouble again. Just how honest did I dare to be? The silence wore on, and I was squirming inside. I decided to risk telling the real truth. "I would have pretended that everything was okay."

"Really! Why?"

"Because if I said anything to you, then you would really hate me. And you would want to help me even less. Then I would be in a mess that kept spiraling downward into more and more pain. I learned early on to keep my mouth shut."

"Where did you learn that?"

"In my family, of course."

"How did they teach you that?"

"By looking at me like they wanted to kill me if I said the wrong thing or by beating me. I knew I couldn't trust them."

"Do you feel you can trust me?"

"Maybe a little bit."

"It takes some trust to be able to say what you just did."

"Yes, it feels risky. In my family I learned that what I *should* say is 'Of course I trust you,' even if I don't."

"As we are talking about this now, does any feeling come up?"

"Not very strongly. I get a little afraid each time I answer you with the truth, but I am getting to trust you, so it's not very intense. It gets very, very clear how dangerous it felt to me in my family."

"What was it like knowing you couldn't trust them?"

"It felt very lonely and very frightening, those same feelings I've been feeling here each day."

"Was there anyone you could trust?"

"My great-grandmother and my aunts from my mother's side of the family."

"What did you trust about them?"

SILENCE

"I never had to wonder if they loved me. It was always obvious."

"And with your parents?"

"I never knew for sure. I was always trying to figure it out."

"But with your great-grandmother and those relatives, there was no question. What were they like?"

"My great-grandmother was just a very serene, quiet person. My aunt, NeNe, was more lively and funny. She loved to tell jokes and gossip, but she was also very peaceful and calm. They lived together in a house that had been in the family for more than forty years."

SILENCE

"Yes?"

"I don't know how to go on from here. I don't feel sad when I talk about them."

"What do you feel?"

"Happy, actually."

"What's wrong with that?"

"Well, I'm supposed to be feeling my feelings."

"Isn't this your feeling?"

"But it doesn't make me want to cry."

"Your happy feelings are just as important as your sad ones, aren't they?"

"I guess so."

"You sound doubtful."

"I am a little bit."

"Why is that?"

"Well, in this therapy, you're supposed to feel and cry."

"And if you don't?"

"Then you aren't a good patient. And you don't get better, and your therapist doesn't like you."

"You don't have to try to make me like you by being a good girl. You've been a good girl all your life. You don't have to do that here." This was said with such a tone of sympathy that I immediately felt intensely sad. She was right. I had spent my life "being good."

"Nobody wants you if you're not good."

"Nobody?"

"Mommy and Daddy don't."

"And what is that like?"

"It's so lonely. I always feel alone, like I have to watch how I behave. And I can't let anyone see how I really am, because then nobody wants me."

"Do you remember a particular time?"

"This seems so trivial, but it really hurt my feelings. I got up early one morning and, trying to be a good girl, I was making breakfast for the little kids without being told. I was just at the end of making scrambled eggs when my father came into the kitchen. He walked over to the stove and looked in the pan. He immediately got furious and told me if I ever cooked eggs like that again he would beat me until I couldn't sit down."

My therapist gasped. "What was he talking about?"

"Because I hadn't put enough butter in the pan, a very thin coating of eggs was sticking to the bottom. So they weren't perfect."

"So you had to be a gourmet chef at what age?"

"Thirteen."

"Seems awfully young to me. Then what happened?"

"Then he put his face really close to mine and said, 'I don't buy food only to have you waste it. Is that clear, young lady?' I just looked at the ground and muttered, 'Yes, Daddy.' Then he said, 'Look at me when I speak to you.' "

SILENCE

"What do you see when you look in his eyes?"

"I don't remember. I don't remember looking up."

"What do you remember?"

"I remember the floor."

78

SILENCE

I could feel myself getting incredibly sad, but I didn't know what to do. Somehow I couldn't cry. I didn't even know exactly what made me sad.

"Let yourself be right there in the room with him. Stay right there. What is happening around you?"

"My brothers and sisters are sitting at the breakfast table. They've all gotten really quiet, which is what we do when Daddy is angry. There's a hush in the room. I'm afraid, and I can feel that they are, too. I'm really afraid to look at him." As I tell her these details I can feel the fear building. It actually feels as if I'm back in that kitchen. "I can smell the eggs, and I can hear the birds in the trees outside the windows. Time feels really slow. Out of the corner of my eye I can see my youngest sister's face. She is looking really worried. That makes me feel even more afraid."

"Stay right there. . . ."

"Everything feels frozen; I can't remember anything else."

"Keep looking. Let the feeling show you the way."

"I see the flower pattern in the linoleum."

"Yes?"

"The background is green but I can't really see." I feel shocked as it all begins to come back. "It's blurry— it's blurry because I'm crying." I started crying and the memory continued to unfurl. "When I do look up, he's looking at me with rage and fury in his eyes. He practically snarls at me as he says, 'Keep that up and I'll really give you something to cry about.' " I cried deeper as the pain struck the middle of my chest. "I'm never good enough. Never, never, never. No matter what I do, it is never good enough. When I try to be good it's not good, and when I'm just plain me it's not good either. I can't stand it. I can't stand it. I cannot stand this anymore." The intensity of the pain was indescribable. I was trapped in a place that I couldn't escape. No matter what action I took or didn't take, I wasn't good enough. I kept crying harder and harder. My chest felt as if two crazed cats were battling it out inside me. The torment and the sorrow kept on and on. I started shouting, "I'm really not bad! I'm not. I'm not. Can't you see how hard I try? Doesn't it matter that I try? I'm just not old enough to be perfect. I try. I try so hard. I try every single day to be good. Can't you love me anyway? Even if I'm not perfectly good? That's what I want. I want you to love me no matter how I am. It would be different if I didn't try. But I do try. I try everything. Please, please love me. I love you. I love you even if *you're* not perfect. I know you aren't good all the time, but I love you anyway. I try to understand. I try to understand you, but you never try with me. You just get angry and hit me or send me out of the room. I would never treat you like that if you were my little boy. I couldn't be that mean to you. I really couldn't. I would be nice and love you a lot. Can't you please just love me? Can't you?" As I thought of him as my little boy, frightened and afraid, looking up at me, the way I was looking at him, I felt sadness overwhelm me. I knew I couldn't hurt him. Why was it so easy for him to hurt me?

"You're mean. You're mean, mean, mean." Each time I said "mean," it felt like exactly the right thing to say, but each time I said it the pain increased. "Don't be mean, Daddy. Please don't be so mean. I don't understand. I cannot understand why you're so mean to me, to all of us." I stopped talking and cried soft sobs in a resigned way. It just seemed I never would understand why he was mean, why it was so easy for him to hurt us. I felt confused as well as sad. Then the realization crept up on me. It hit hard. "You just don't love me, do you? You really and truly don't." As that horrible insight struck me like a brick I started crying harder and harder. "Nobody loves me. Nobody loves me. Nobody. Nobody. Nobody."

I cried and sobbed. I felt completely alone. It felt that there was no one, not one single person in the world who loved me or cared about me at all. The harder I cried the more I had to cry about. I couldn't get away from that feeling no matter what I did. I squirmed and rolled; I covered my face with the pillow; but I kept on crying. As I cried, more insights crashed into realization. If Daddy didn't love me— hated me, in fact, because I wasn't perfect—that meant no other person could love me either. I felt I had to hide. I couldn't let my therapist see me. I crawled around the side of the sofa and hid. I was still crying with all my heart; the muscles of my belly hurt from the intensity of my sobs. Hidden, I began my litany again: "Nobody loves me. Nobody loves me. Nobody. Nobody will ever love me." It felt all too true. I cried and cried and cried. I couldn't stop. Tears poured down my face and I could hardly breathe for the mucus blocking my nose. I began groping around the floor, trying to find tissues. I opened my eyes to see my therapist gently pushing the box in my direction. She looked sad. This led to a new burst of crying because it was really clear that in fact she *didn't* hate me, too. I blew my nose and began to talk to her through my sobbing. "I can't believe it. He really doesn't love me. It makes it feel like everyone hates me. That no one could possibly care about me, ever."

"Tell him."

"You make me feel unlovable. It's not just you who can't love me. It feels like no one could ever, ever, ever love me in a thousand years. And I feel slimy and stupid, that there is no hope for me. Now I feel ashamed of myself. And all because the eggs stuck to the pan! I feel I have to hide. I can't let anyone see me. Because they'll see the same thing you see. They'll see and know that I'm a dirty, stupid, ugly little girl who can't do anything right. Everything about me is wrong and I can't change it! This is how I am. No matter how hard I try I can't, can't, can't be different. I can't be the way you like. Even when I try. I give up. I give up." As I said those words a feeling of hopelessness descended upon me. A black wave of sadness, even despair, washed over me again and again. I cried from the bottom of my heart. I moaned and sobbed. I felt sentenced to misery forever. "I give up," I said again and again and again. Those were the exact, proper, and fitting words for my feeling. Each time I repeated that phrase, I dropped deeper and deeper into a black hole of sadness. I knew I could never be as he wanted. Because he didn't want me. He didn't want to care about me, he *didn't* want to love me.

As I cried more and more deeply, my emotional focus shifted. All those years of struggling and trying to be wanted, to be good—wasted, pointless. The light came on. *He would never love me.* The words changed then. "I give up on you, Daddy." I continued crying, but almost with a sense of relief. I could feel myself letting go of the cord of feeling that tied us together, the cord of that useless struggle to change into someone he could love. It would never be. I had been fighting off knowing this for my entire life. And although the knowledge hurt so deeply, accepting it was like lancing a boil—painful, but also an exquisite relief. "I give up on *you*, Daddy." The way I was crying changed. No longer all that furious energy and noise, it settled into a low and steady cry. I was winding down. "You'll never be the daddy that loves me and cares about me. The daddy I always wanted. The kind one, the sweet, gentle one. I can stop trying, and I've tried so hard, so very hard." This led to a renewed burst of loud sobbing for all that wasted effort. "You don't know how to love anyone. You don't love me. You don't love Mommy. You don't love the dog. You don't love anybody."

My crying then softened more and more. Soon I was lying in a state of total quiet and peacefulness. It went on and on. Many thoughts trailed through my mind—the different things I had done in my life with him and others trying to be loved and liked. Pointless. I didn't feel sad now, but at peace. It seemed I had been trying not to know this for so long, and now I knew. My father couldn't and wouldn't ever love me.

My awareness of the room and my therapist slowly drifted back into focus. I had completely forgotten about her; this encounter had been totally between me and my father. No one else had been there, just the two of us. I looked up at my therapist. She looked completely relaxed as well, with her hands folded in her lap.

"I'm back," I said with a little chuckle. I felt giddy, almost light-headed.

"Where have you been?"

"It feels like I took a time machine back to the nineteen sixties."

"You went all the way back, didn't you?"

"It seemed as if I could eat the eggs again, it was that real."

"How are you feeling now?"

"I feel a bit light-headed."

"Sometimes that happens when you feel very intensely. It just takes a little time to recover. Would you like to talk about it?"

"Actually, I feel like being quiet for a while."

"Take all the time you need."

I put my head back on the pillow and just let my mind wander. It was pretty direct wandering, though.

I kept thinking of the moment when I could feel myself give up on my father. It had been extremely painful, but after the pain had come an intense relief. Then suddenly, I began to doubt myself. Could it possibly be this easy? Just a few hours of crying, and suddenly the pain of years is gone? I turned to my therapist again. "I'm starting to wonder if there is something wrong with this. Is it really possible that this is all over with my father? It seems too easy. Won't I ever have to cry about this again?"

"I only wish that were true. You don't erase this much pain in a few sessions. This is the beginning of a process, the process of being in touch with your feelings and being able to feel deeply. The tentacles of this pain reach into many areas of your life. Some you haven't even realized yet. Many of those strands of pain have to be felt on an individual basis over a long time for lasting change to take place. Many different situations in your daily life can bring up this same pain, and when that happens you will have the possibility of dealing with it in a new way, by feeling it back to the source. Sometimes I think of it like those old-time wagon wheels. There are many different spokes but they all lead back to the hub."

"That makes sense. I was wondering if this was a fantasy relief, because I couldn't see myself getting over this so quickly."

"You're right. Healing takes time. If you have a badly infected wound that hasn't been treated, you get an amazing sense of relief when you clean the infected spot and start using antibiotics; but if you don't continue to clean and treat the infection, healing doesn't take place—or at least not as rapidly as it could. This is not a magical miracle cure—one application and all is well. It takes continuing hard work and courage."

"The more I think about it, the more I am sure that my courage comes from my great-grandmother. Daddy was so frightening that I think I would have been a much more cowardly person without her. There was such a contrast in the way the two of them treated me. Without her I think I really would have believed completely that I was all bad. As it was I almost completely believed it, but there was always a tiny, tiny little voice that said, 'He's wrong.' "

"That's a very important voice. It's your real self talking to you. In the course of therapy, that voice gets louder and you get to trust and believe it more."

"Does everyone have that voice?"

"I think everyone does, but for some people the volume of their pain is so loud that they can barely hear it. With feeling and learning to listen to that interior voice, it gets much clearer. You know, I was wondering if you had any thoughts on how this feeling has affected you."

"When I was lying quiet there for so long I had a lot of thoughts about that. The biggest effect that I can see is that I have been incredibly afraid whenever I try something that I can't do perfectly right off. The fear of not being perfect and the horrible consequences of imperfection have stopped me from doing so many things. For instance, I've been terri-fied to learn how to drive. And it's a horrible ordeal whenever someone tries to teach me something. I get so frightened and defensive that I can hardly hear what's being said to me. In addition to being afraid of what that other person thinks of me, I'm afraid of what goes on inside me. I suddenly start saying things to myself like, 'You're stupid, too stupid to learn this; you're an idiot; you're just wasting this person's time; of course they hate you,' and on and on and on. I love dancing, and I haven't danced since I was about twelve years old. Why? Because there's a period of time when you're learning a new dance when you're just not good at it. And in that time I feel so ugly, stu-pid, and disgusting that I can't stand it."

"It sounds like this feeling made it impossible for you to do things that you really very much want to do."

"That's it."

"Well, when you think about those things now—dancing, for instance—how do you feel?"

"I was just checking inside myself and funnily enough it feels a little better. It still seems scary, but it also feels like it's possible."

"I often say something similar, that feeling your pain takes the impossible and makes it possible—extremely difficult sometimes, but possible nonethe-less. Keep that in mind for the future: one action you can take to help bring up your feelings and give you back something you enjoy would be to go to a dance or to take some lessons. A lot of pain might come up, but the payoff would eventually be worth it."

"Okay."

"I was thinking about something you said yesterday. Remember telling me that you get frightened to take risks?"

"Yes, I do."

"In the feeling you had today you took a risk by deciding to cook the eggs. Then look how your father responded. He attacked you."

"Exactly. That's what I'm afraid of, that I'll be punished instead of him being happy with me."

"I can clearly see that would make you want to do the safe thing at all times."

"That's something I hope will change in therapy, because many times the safe thing isn't what I really want to do."

"That can change, but as I keep saying, over time. First you might take small risks, then bigger ones for things that are important to you."

"You mean I'm not going to save the world tomorrow?" I asked with a smile.

"Not quite that soon," she laughed. "Maybe next week. Is there anything else you would like to talk about today?"

"I kept reminding myself to talk about my great-grandmother, but somehow that slipped away today."

"That can happen. You have a plan of what you want to talk about or feel and something more powerful or more spontaneous intervenes. It's better to let that happen than to try to control your feelings. This is a process, and you will have the opportunity to talk about all the things that are important to you over time. If you'd like you can talk about her now; we haven't devoted that much time to her and it seems she was a pivotal person in your life."

"I would like to do that. Some of the best times of my life were when we went to visit her."

"Why don't you talk about going to her house to visit and tell me all the things you can remember."

"There were big chestnut trees planted all along the street leading up to their house. I remember peeling the bark from the tree in front of their house. There were hydrangea bushes planted on either side of the front steps, with a brick walkway leading up to the screened front porch. On the porch was a porch swing suspended from the ceiling that I loved to ride in, and there was a glider sofa. My MaMa had a rocking chair that she always sat in on the front porch. In the cool of the evening we would all sit out there and drink lemonade in tall glasses. When we came to visit, someone would always be sitting on the front porch waiting for us to arrive. My father would pull into the driveway and honk the horn once. The porch door would fly open and NeNe and MaMa would be there beside the car, hugging and kissing us and saying how big we had grown. Everyone would be talking at once, and even my father would be smiling. Once we went inside we would all head for the kitchen, where there would be piles of fried chicken or apple pie or doughnuts for us to eat. It was completely informal; with Daddy, we always had to sit at the table and be good. At MaMa's we could carry food into the backyard or out on the porch, and it was fine with them. The feeling of the house was always warm. The thing I remember most is that I wasn't afraid of anyone who lived there. That was such a change from being around Daddy. One year when we made our annual trip to visit down south, MaMa told my parents she thought I seemed really too tired for a twelve-year-old and she thought they should leave me down there with them for the summer rather than go home at the end of the two weeks. I don't know how she did it, but she convinced them, and I was allowed to stay there for an extra month. It was the happiest time of my life. I had never had such a peaceful time. I was never afraid in that house. No one ever hit me! That was so amazing to me. I believe that was one of the times I got the sense that something was wrong with Daddy and not with me."

"That was such an important thing for you to find out."

"It truly was. I think I'd like to stop now. I feel very tired and I just wanted to talk about my great-grandmother, but I think I've had enough for today."

"All right, I'll see you tomorrow at our regular time."

Session Six

The Patient Speaks

PHYSICALLY, I FELT LIGHT-HEADED LEAVING MY
session, though emotionally I felt open and extremely vulnerable. I was glad that I didn't have to go
to school or a job immediately after experiencing
such a very deep feeling. I didn't feel prepared to
deal with other people. As I walked along, I kept remembering all the things I hadn't been able to allow
myself to do, things that felt just too risky—like
singing with other people, though I have a very good
voice, or dancing, or riding a bicycle, or even accepting the four-year scholarship I had won to college.
All of these things had been impossible for me because I was so afraid. I hadn't even noticed how
frightened I was, since I'd felt that way for as long as I
could remember.

The thought that I hadn't gone to college because I knew I wouldn't be good enough kept pounding in my head. The fact that I'd won an academic scholarship didn't make any difference. I'd left that college after such a short time because I was sure I wouldn't measure up. And I was terrified that everyone would find out. I felt like crying all over again. It felt so sad that I couldn't do what I wanted and what I was capable of doing because of my childhood. Then I thought of my purpose in coming to therapy. I wanted to change all that, and hopefully, over time I could. With that, I felt better and began to notice the sun and the wonderful smell of jasmine wafting through the air. This definitely seemed the right thing to be doing.

As I walked along I found myself checking inside myself to see if I felt "cured" yet. Unfortunately, I didn't. However, when I let myself wonder if any small changes had taken place, I noticed that there were some differences. I actually didn't feel as shy as usual on the street; at this moment, I wasn't concerned with what the passing people were thinking of me. As I stepped into a coffee shop to have some lunch I noted with surprise that I wasn't too tense at being there alone, that it wasn't too hard to get the words out to order my food. All right, I thought, I wasn't all better but this was definitely an improvement. I felt pretty good. And while I was sitting quietly in the restaurant that light-headed feeling passed.

Therapy was starting to feel like an exciting adventure, a voyage of discovery to find myself—the self I'd lost or hidden away so long ago. It seemed that bits of me were hidden in the smallest places like the glance of a woman on the street, or how I felt sitting in the room with my therapist. It struck me that after feeling so vulnerable, I was starting to feel sturdy. That was a new sensation. And I liked the feeling. I was wondering why the waitress didn't seem so intimidating, and I suddenly realized that the frightened feeling I usually got in restaurants had very little to do with the people there and everything to do with Daddy. I had been expecting everyone to be as angry as he was and as frightening. It was as if the "Daddy" feeling had peeled away from other people. It belonged with him, and during my session I'd put it back where it belonged. I had an image of me hiding the truth about Daddy in my feelings of fear of other people. At the moment, he seemed scarier than at any time since childhood, but the other people around me felt amazingly neutral. I went out into the street from the restaurant and checked my responses and awareness. As cars drove by I didn't feel that the people inside them were laughing at me or about to jump out and hurt me. It was *now* when I didn't have those feelings that I became acutely aware of how prevalent they usually were for me! I walked on, basking in the ease I felt. This was a completely unique experience.

After arriving back in my room I spent a lot of time writing up the session and its aftermath in my diary. It seemed so important to record and acknowledge what I had felt and realized. Somehow the experience seemed more definite and more permanent once it was written there, in my diary, in my handwriting. I realized that it felt as if it could slip away or be forgotten. I tried to promise myself that I would not forget. As I made that promise to myself, I remembered that I had promised that same thing as a child. Only then it had been a silent threat to my father: "I will not forget how mean you've been. I will always remember what you did and I won't ever be like you." I was struck by how important promises were to me—the promises I made and the ones others made as well. It felt as if that childhood promise had helped me be true to myself.

As I put my diary away, I noticed a little packet of my childhood photos. I had brought them along to help me remember being little. I had a little laugh at myself over that; I certainly didn't seem to be having much trouble remembering. As I looked at the photos, other memories came back. Two in particular stayed with me.

One photo was of me and my brother; in it I was about two and a half years old and he was about one. I looked very sweet and relaxed and happy; in fact we both did. It was a studio shot, done by a good friend of my parents who was a professional photographer and took lots of our family photos. My brother was wearing a little ruffled shirt. He looked very cute, with really big ears that stuck out on the sides of his head. The amazing thing was that he looked completely peaceful, whereas now he's always nervous and jittery, biting his fingernails and twisting his hair. In the photo he has the calmest, most gentle smile on his face. It was sad to realize what he had lost. Then my eye strayed over to look at myself. I also looked incredibly calm, peaceful, and gentle. I had little chubby cheeks and a natural, easy smile, not one of those forced "cheese" grins that I developed later. There was such a contrast to the frightened, tense person I grew up to be. In the second photo, my first-grade school picture, I was dressed in my favorite dress, which I still remember. It was navy blue with pink trim, and had a flounce along the bottom that was also pink. I remembered feeling especially pretty in that dress, but that wasn't the feeling reflected in that photo. My lips were pursed and I looked into the camera with determination and utter seriousness. I did not look like a child, but like an adult locked in a small body. It made me really sad to see the contrast between those two photos. I almost cried but somehow I couldn't. I put the pictures away after deciding I'd take them with me for my next session.

In the morning I woke with the sense of a dream but try as I might to hold on to them, the images slipped away like water into desert sand. I was wide awake and of course wondering where this therapy journey would take me today. I wasn't very hungry, so after eating a piece of fruit I went outside and started walking around. I felt a little guilty, at first, but my therapist had explained that the restrictions on my activities were not a punishment but rather to provide the quiet time necessary to allow feelings to arise. She had further explained that I would come to an understanding of when and how I used my free time as a defense—to prevent myself feeling things I didn't want to feel and be aware of—and when for true enjoyment. I checked myself inside and, as I felt really very well, decided to go for the walk. I felt a lingering sense of possibly doing wrong, but I went out anyway.

Thinking about my slightly guilty feeling began a trail of questions. Why did I so rarely feel completely comfortable with the decisions I made? Why was there constant mind chatter, questioning, doubting, wondering, analyzing? It was going on right that very minute: "Are you sure this is all right? Maybe you're doing the wrong thing. You should go back to the room right now. What if you are defending against some feelings and you don't know it? You could be, you know. You're new at this, and you don't know very much. She could be really angry with you. You'd better be careful. You could get into big trouble." And on and on. It came almost as a shock when I actually *listened* to what was going on in my head. And this was a time when I felt good! I decided this was definitely something I would need to talk about.

By the time I actually went to my session, I was feeling pretty confused. I had enjoyed the beginning of my walk, but hearing how I usually spoke to myself internally made me feel overwhelmed.

"Where should I start?" I asked my therapist.

"Take your time," my therapist said, "and let yourself see where you are."

"Everything wants to come out in a mad rush, and I'm not sure where to begin."

SILENCE

As I lay there quietly, feeling no pressure from my therapist, things began to get clearer. "I don't trust myself. I began to notice it today when I had to decide for myself whether to stay in my room and be a 'good girl' or go out for a walk."

"Mmm-hmm."

"I went out for the walk, but the whole time I was questioning myself about whether or not I'd made the right decision, if you'd be angry, perhaps I was defending, this could be the wrong thing to do, and more and more thoughts and questions. What made it really bad was realizing that I do this all the time and that I was actually doing it *less* than usual because I am feeling pretty good right now. I was also noticing how frightened I am, have always been. It seems that my awareness of my fear is increasing. I used to think I was physically afraid, but now I see I'm afraid of what I think, even *how* I think. I hate this sense that nothing feels secure and easy. Everything feels so hard, so full of danger and the possibility of pain. I just wish I could get away from it all, that I could make it all disappear and not be here."

"I can understand you wanting that."

"No matter how much I want it, though, it doesn't come."

"No, that takes some time of working on yourself and feeling what drives those thoughts and fears."

"I feel so upset."

"Upset?"

"Yes, I feel sad and nervous at the same time."

"Sad and nervous?"

"Yes, like I want to cry and jump out of my skin at the same time."

"Can you pinpoint exactly what it is that does that to you?"

"It's something about deciding on my own to go outside for a walk without permission."

"Without permission?"

"I had to get permission to do anything in my family. If I wanted to open the refrigerator, go outside, eat food, talk on the telephone, I had to get permission."

"So how did you feel when you left your room without permission this morning?"

I felt myself get afraid when she asked that question. Then it filtered through my confusion that she didn't sound angry. "I felt fine when I first left, but then as I walked around I got more and more upset. One part of it is being afraid that you'll be angry with me, but the other part is feeling so sorry for myself that I have to be afraid, that I have to second-guess something so small as going out for a walk. And I knew it would be okay with you, since you said I would start to know myself if I was defending against feelings. I wasn't defending, but somehow it seemed that I could be doing the wrong thing. It drives me crazy!"

"What if it did make me angry?"

Oh, no! Maybe she really was angry!? What could I do now? "It would make me very scared."

"Yes?"

SILENCE

This was really getting bad now. I could feel my heart going faster, my breath coming quicker as well.

"What do you want to say to me?"

"Please don't be angry."

SILENCE

"You sound very frightened as you say that."

"I really am." I could hear the little quaver in my voice.

"Tell me."

"I'm frightened. I'm really scared you'll be angry because I did the wrong thing."

"What if I am?"

Now I got even more scared. "You'll hate me and you'll throw me out of therapy without letting me explain."

"What do you want to explain?"

"I thought it was okay. I didn't mean to do anything wrong. Please don't be angry. Please don't kick me out of therapy. Please don't hate me." I started crying, feeling scared and sad. I felt small, helpless, and unwanted. Soon I felt so frightened at the thought of her anger that I couldn't let myself cry.

"It's okay," she said, "this leads somewhere important. Trust your feeling and see where it goes." She touched me lightly on the shoulder.

"I feel scared. It's really dangerous if I don't do exactly what I'm supposed to. I get hated and I get hit." I started crying all over again. I kept my eyes closed and thought of her sitting behind me, hating me and being furiously angry with me for going out of the motel room. It made me cry harder and harder. The more I cried the more it seemed that what I had done wasn't such a bad thing. That started a whole new line of pain. Why was I so hated for doing small things wrong? What was so bad about doing what I felt like doing? My crying vacillated between, "Please don't be angry" and "I'm not so bad, why do you hate me?" I shot a quick look at my therapist's face. She was looking sad, too! This made me cry even more. *She* didn't hate me. "You don't really hate me, do you?"

"No, I don't."

I believed her. But I was still stuck with that horrible pain inside. "I'm still hurting, even though I believe you."

"Who hated you and hit you when you did the wrong thing? Who didn't let you explain?"

"Daddy never did. He would say, 'I don't want to hear your explanation. You did it and now you have to suffer the consequences.' "

"When did you feel this same way with him?"

Suddenly, just like all the other times, the whole

scene scrolled before my eyes, just like a movie. Only I was the movie. I was six years old and had gone to the neighborhood grocery store in our small southern town to buy something for my dad. It was Mother's rule that if the coins in the change included exactly one penny I could spend the penny; if there was more than one penny, all the change had to be brought back to her. On that day, glory of glories, there was one penny of change! I spent a few seconds choosing a piece of candy, then happily walked home, munching away. I skipped up the front steps and gave Daddy his package and the rest of his change. As I turned to walk away he said, "Where's my penny?"

I turned back and said, "I spent the penny."

In a deep, ominous, very quiet voice, he said, "Who told you to do that?"

"I thought it was okay, because Mother always—"

"Who told *you* you could think?" he furiously interrupted me.

"But Daddy, Mother always lets me—"

"I don't care what your mother does. I want that penny. Now."

Now I started crying. "I already ate the candy. I can't get the penny back."

"I'll just have to take it out of your hide, then, won't I?" He spit the words from his mouth.

I cried even harder. "Please, Daddy, I won't—"

"Crying won't help you now. Get inside and pull your pants down. I'll be in for you in a minute."

My mother walked out onto the porch, obviously

having heard everything. "I'll give you your penny," she said to my father.

"I don't want your penny; I want her to learn a lesson."

"I always let her spend one penny," my mother answered.

"I don't care what *you* do, *I* don't let her do that."

My head had been whipping back and forth between the two of them. Everything depended on whether she could reason with him. I watched the rage on his face increasing with every word she said. Her expression had gone from calm to dismay to anger in turn.

"Be reasonable," Mother almost shouted at him. "It was an honest mistake."

"She has a lesson to learn, and I'm going to teach it to her." He shot a hard look at me. "Didn't I tell you to get inside and wait for me?"

I left immediately. As I walked through the living room, the other kids sat frozen, like statues of fear. They all looked at me with their eyes wide open. One of my brothers wiggled his fingers at me as I went by. I went into my room and sat on the bed. I could hear my parents continuing to argue, though I couldn't hear what was being said. I got more and more afraid as I sat there. I could tell from their voice tones that my mother was losing the argument. Hers was getting more quiet and pleading, and Daddy's louder and more violent. He would be coming in to beat me soon. Next I heard the slamming of the screen door and the loud clump of his footsteps coming down the hall. My heart beat faster and faster. He swung the door open and stepped into the room.

I had a last-minute thought of trying, again, to explain, beg, or plead for mercy. One look at his face made the words die in my throat. His eyes were squinting, his lips pressed tightly together. He gave a little smirky smile as he began to undo his belt. "Well, young lady, are you ready?" I couldn't help myself; I started begging and crying anyway, even though it was useless. "Please, please, Daddy, Daddy, I'll be good. I promise." That little smile of his broke out again. "It's too late for that now. You should have thought of that before you spent that money."

He pointed for me to lie down across my bed. I assumed the position: the top part of my body, bent at the hips, lying on the bed, with my knees on the floor and my bottom sticking up. I waited for the whistling sound of his webbed belt slicing through the air. I bit the bedcovers and held on tightly with my hands. I wished I could get out of my body, out of the room, out of the house. But there was no escape for me. The sound of the belt flashing toward me ended all thought. Time sped up and slowed down at the same time. He was hitting me with all his might, ordering me to be still, and talking to me at the same time. "You won't forget this soon, will you? Will you? You'll remember this!" Shrieking and crying, I tried to answer him. I was twisting and turning on the bed, trying to find some way not to be hurt. There was no way. The pain of the blows was like fire, burning and searing my skin. My body, without my consciously thinking of it, tried to get away. I scrabbled across the bed, wedging myself against the wall. I drummed my legs on the bed, screaming for help. None came. He hit my back, my bottom, my legs. In my terror I wet myself. He beat me more for that. I was sure he was killing me. Even worse than the physical pain was the knowledge that he *wanted* to hurt me. He *liked* doing it. I could hear the laughter in his voice as he told me how much more this hurt him than me.

"You won't steal any more of my money, will you!" He was hitting me and talking at the same time. When I didn't answer immediately, he hit me harder and faster. "Answer me!" I didn't even know what I was supposed to say. I just shouted out "No" or "Yes" as fast as I could. Then he beat me for that. "Oh, you're going to do it again, are you? Well, you haven't learned your lesson yet!" And again he beat me harder. Everything inside and outside hurt. My heart was bursting with sadness, and my body was writhing in pain. I cried and sobbed.

As I came to myself, I found my body pressed up against the wall of the therapy room in the same position of my childhood beating. I slowly looked around the room and saw my therapist looking almost as disheveled as I felt. Her hands were clasped tightly in her lap, but her hair was spiking up on her head. She looked sweaty and tired. "Wow," was all I could say.

"Welcome back," she replied.

Shifting onto my back, I gave a deep sigh. Strangely, I felt completely calm and relaxed, but I didn't have anything to say. The silence deepened, and I let my thoughts, slow as they were, drift. It was as clear as crystal. The reason I had been so worried about going for the walk was this very feeling! I had learned, very deeply, that any decision I made on my own, without higher authority, was very dangerous. Hadn't my father said, "Who told *you* you could think?"

"The reason I was so afraid was this very feeling with Daddy. It was dangerous, with him, to make any decisions on my own. I think he actually *looked* for reasons to beat me."

"From what I saw from the outside, this was a very intense feeling, but I don't know what actually happened. Please tell me."

That was a shock. I had been so deeply in my feeling that I assumed she knew everything I did. As I told her the story of the feeling she was mostly quiet, occasionally making a few sympathetic sounds.

"How did it feel when you realized your father wanted to hurt you?"

"That was what hurt me the most. It was more painful than the beating. If he wants to hurt me that means he really, really doesn't love me. I don't have a father." As I said those words, the tears started again. Deep boo-hoos and sobs poured out, expressing a sadness that couldn't be put into words. This time I wasn't in the past; this was me now, the adult, mourning my loss: "I never will have the daddy I want, the kind, loving one who protects and comforts me." I thought as I cried that I had never been comforted by my father. Not once in my entire life. He was always the one I feared and avoided. I turned onto my stomach, clutching the pillow for comfort. This crying was steady, sad, and slow. It was like crying about someone who had died long ago. And in a way, this was a death. It was the death of my hopes and illusions about my father. I was slowly accepting the reality, the sad truth of my childhood. Wiping my eyes and blowing my nose, I turned back to my therapist. "I thought I was all finished for today," I said ruefully.

"Sometimes our feelings surprise us."

"Feeling this makes me lonely and frightened because I need him to protect me from scary things and people, only he's the scariest person I know."

"No wonder it was so frightening for you to decide to do what you wanted, when you wanted. That feeling must affect many areas of your life."

"Well, I hardly ever feel completely certain that what I've decided to do is the right thing. I nearly always agonize over my decisions either before or after and sometimes both! It was really frightening for me to decide to come to therapy, especially since I had to travel three thousand miles to get here and give up all my friends and family. Nearly everyone I know was against me doing it. All I had to go on was the feeling of hope I had gotten from the book. I was terrified on the airplane coming out here and if I'd been able to take an immediate return flight by staying on the plane I'm sure I would have gone home."

"How are you feeling about that decision now?"

"It feels more and more right. And what happened today only confirms that for me. It is still amazing to me that something that happened so long ago could still be affecting me now. I thought that when I grew up all these events from my childhood would just fall away."

"Too bad that's not true. Then no one would need therapy."

Session Seven

The Therapist's Voice

As I DID MY USUAL START-OF-DAY ROUTINE—
answering calls, watering the plant, reading through
my case notes—I was occupied with thoughts of my
new patient. She'd had six days of deep, intense feeling, and I was fairly certain that at today's session she
would be tired, maybe even resistant to more feeling.
After feeling so often and deeply, I'd noticed with
myself and other people, that often there would
need to be a rest day, time when the person just did
not have the energy necessary to have a deep, connected feeling. I was still considering my patient's
likely state of mind when she arrived.

   She came in differently than she had the day before. This time she fairly bounced into the room,
exuding energy. She settled quickly, finding a com-

fortable position. There was still a slight chill in the air and she covered herself with the blanket that was always in the room.

"I slept really well last night," she started off, "and I had a neat dream."

"Great."

"Would you like to hear it?"

"Would you like to tell it?"

"I just wondered if it was okay to talk about something other than my feelings. You know, things that aren't important."

"Aren't your dreams important to you?"

"Yes, they are. I didn't know if they would be important here."

"What's important to you *is* the important stuff here."

SILENCE

"That has never been true before," she eventually said in a surprised tone.

"I guess that's why you're here."

"So, yes, I would like to tell my dream."

"I'm all ears."

"I don't remember all of the dream, but this is what stayed with me. I've walked through a dark forest, with overhanging trees—"

"Tell it as if it's happening now," I interrupt her to say. This could more easily allow feelings to arise. "Let yourself be right there."

"I'm walking through a dark forest, with branches overhanging the path I'm on. I'm not sure where the path leads, but I keep walking along. The woods have a slightly sinister atmosphere to them and I think to myself that I wouldn't like to stay in them overnight. As I continue, the overgrowth gets less dense and light starts to break through the tops of the trees; the nature of the forest begins to change. From an all-pine forest it begins to be mixed with taller, airier trees like maples and oaks. I'm liking the feel of it much better. It eventually leads to an open grassy area leading up to a cottage that looks like it's from olden times. I really like this place. The back door is standing open. I go to the door and call out. No one answers. I step through the doorway into a cozy kitchen. I call out again and still no one answers. As I step further into the kitchen I notice an open trap-door in the center of the floor. I am drawn to it and go over and start down the dark, winding steps. It's very dimly lit, but there is enough light to see my way down the stairs. It's a bit scary but something draws me on. As I go deeper I begin to understand or re-member that this is *my* house and these are *my* stairs that I'm walking down. It's a narrow space, but I be-gin to feel quite comfortable. I keep going down and I begin to see small, round, multicolored stained glass windows embedded in the stone walls of the staircase. They are so beautiful that they almost make me cry. Shafts of warm blue and red light are gleam-ing up from the bottom of the staircase. As I descend further I begin to see small chests strewn about the floor. Stepping closer I see jewels, loose stones, strings and ropes of pearls. They are unbelievably beautiful. Looking around, I also see that the space continues, with rooms leading off rooms and many branching hallways. I wake up as I think, These are mine, too."

SILENCE

I wait to see if there's anything she wants to volunteer. Eventually I ask, "How do you feel?"

"I feel good. I like that dream so much. It leaves me with the same feeling as fairy tales I used to read when I was young."

"How so?"

"In the fairy tales the good ones always get their just deserts. They get rewarded for being good. It felt wonderful in the dream when I realized that all that beauty, all those bright colors were mine. It makes me feel like crying."

"You said that as you were telling the dream, too. What about it brings up that feeling?"

"It's a kind of happy feeling of sadness, a sweet pain feeling. . . . We were always poor. And I was nearly always afraid. In my imagination and the worlds of my books were the only places that things were nice, that it was possible to be happy for days on end, rather than just moments, the way it was in real life. I know it's just a dream, but it feels so nice."

"Dreams can point out to us the way we really feel about certain things. I wouldn't say this is 'just a dream.' Let yourself go back to that moment in your dream."

SILENCE

"I feel my dream is telling me something about myself. It's telling me that there's something valuable deep inside, that I have to go really deep to find it."

"Yes?" I asked.

"I kept thinking about the dream on the way over. Every time I think of the windows and the jewels I get very happy. It feels like the dream is talking about my therapy. That therapy is the way I can use to go down deep, scary stairs to find the treasure of myself."

"That really is a neat dream. You must have felt very good when you woke up from it."

"I did. And I woke up differently than I normally do. Usually I wake up with a jolt—suddenly I am awake and completely alert. This morning I seemed to slide awake, almost like coming up through warm water into the air."

"That sounds much more gentle."

"Yes, it's in such contrast to what I'm used to. So many times everything feels rough and rushed. This dream felt magical."

"That seems to be very important to you. I noticed you mentioned fairy tales earlier." I knew there was something about the dream we had to go back to since she had mentioned feeling like crying, but I also knew we had to do it in her rhythm.

"It is. I remember that from the time I was very young I would read fairy tales for comfort. Good always triumphed in those stories, not like in my real life, where the bad, like Daddy, got away with everything."

"What else do you remember about reading those tales?"

"It's funny you ask that because now something I hadn't remembered in a very long time is coming back to me. My favorite fairy-tale books were named after colors; there was one called *The Blue Fairy Book*, and another was *The Pink Fairy Book*. I would go up into the room I shared with my sisters and I'd roll up in a blue satin down comforter that MaMa had made for me. That comforter was really precious to me. I called it 'my blue cover,' from when I was really little. When I was rolled up inside there I felt loved and comforted." Her voice had softened; she was speaking in an almost sleepy tone. She had suited her actions to the words and had rolled up completely in the office blanket. Matching my voice to hers I said, "Can you let yourself go back there?"

SILENCE

SILENCE

I heard little sniffles coming from inside the blanket. She went on for some time, then came out, blowing her nose with a little smile. "It's that same feeling of 'sweet pain' I was telling you about from my dream. My favorite story from the fairy tales was one called 'Snakes and Toads and Pearls and Diamonds.' It's all about two sisters, one good and one bad. The good one has to do all the work and is treated very badly by her family. The bad one doesn't do any work and is the mother's favorite. Separately they each meet a woman who is thirsty and hungry. The good one shares with her and is rewarded by having pearls and diamonds pour from her lips each time she speaks. The bad one refuses to share and is mean besides. Her punishment is that snakes and frogs drop from her lips as she speaks. When I went back just now I remembered how I promised myself that one day good things would happen to me because I tried to be good. There is a connecting link between that fairy tale and my dream; it's being rewarded with jewels. In my dream I find out that what's inside me is valuable and beautiful." Tears begin rolling down her face.

"What's the sadness?"

"That for so long I didn't remember. That for so long I really believed I was bad inside, just because of how I was treated. It feels sad but good at the same time. Now I am beginning to feel differently. Thank you, MaMa, for loving me enough so I could start to remember." She cried a few more soft, gentle sobs, then stopped.

SILENCE

"It's so funny. I felt so good that I really didn't think I was going to cry at all today. And I never would have dreamed that I would cry about something good."

"Feelings never cease to amaze."

"You can say that again. Rubies and diamonds and pearls, oh my! What an image. This is a dream I won't forget in a hurry. I feel so good. I'm so glad I didn't forget this dream. It feels like a sign from inside myself that I'm on the right track."

"There's nothing better than having that inner certainty, is there?"

"I haven't had it so many times that I can remember, but I sure like how it feels," she said with a hearty laugh. "I know our time isn't up," she said, "but I feel so good I'd really like to go do something fun. Is that okay?"

"What do you feel?"

"I'm not so sure."

"Having trouble trusting your judgment again?"

"Yes, I think that's it. Today has been so easy and I feel so good. I think there has to be something wrong with it."

"Take a risk and say what feels like the right thing to do." I really wanted to help her become more aware of the fact that she did know what was best for her.

She took a big breath, then said, "I think I feel like stopping right now. I really do feel good. And I'm tired, but it's a relaxed, peaceful tired. I feel as if I could do absolutely nothing . . . and enjoy it."

"Trust that feeling, since the whole point of going through all this pain is to get to feel good again. I say—go do it! And remember that somewhere inside you, you *always* know what is right for you. You've been taught not to listen to that small inner voice, but it is there and you can hear it."

She took my hand in both of hers, looked me in the eye, and said, "Thanks."

"You are most welcome." As she left I thought that her dream had provided her with beautiful symbols of what she had inside, as well as the perfect feeling to allow her to rest.

Session Eight

The Therapist's Voice

MY USUAL MORNING ACTIVITIES HAD BEEN DIS-
rupted by an early morning call that required my immediate attention. With my schedule thrown off, I
found myself hurrying into the Institute, with just
moments to spare before the arrival of my patient. I
didn't have my accustomed free time to contem-
plate, or even consider, how she might be feeling, on
this, her last day of the three-week intensive.

"I've been thinking of all I've learned during this
time," my patient said as she came into the room.

"What have you learned?" I asked.

She paused, thinking. After a few moments she
said, "The most important thing to me at the moment, besides starting to learn how to let my feelings
out, is that I'm beginning to get a tiny glimmer of a

feeling of myself inside." She patted her chest as she said this. "It used to feel so empty in here. Now it feels there is a small piece of me beginning to grow. I don't really know how to put it into words. Remember my dream? The one about going down into the lower levels and finding my treasure? The treasure of myself? Well, I feel that a piece of that brightly colored light about the size of a few grains of sand is right inside the middle of my chest. It feels really tiny, but it is there."

"What a beautiful image. It's curious, your saying that, because I sometimes tell people that every time they have a feeling, or tell the truth about who they are, or are true to what they really feel inside, they get a piece of themselves back."

"That's exactly what I feel—that minute pieces of the real me, the way I most truly am, are joining together again after being blasted apart by my life."

SILENCE

She began to speak again. "I just had a scary thought. What happens when you *don't* feel and you *aren't* true to yourself?"

"What do you think?"

"I'm afraid that it can all slip away. That in a flash I can go back to feeling totally confused and empty."

"Of course you can be confused and feel empty sometimes, because those feelings are part of life. And you have had more than your fair share of them due to your childhood. This process of change will take some time, since you can't undo years of confusion and pain in a short time. The point is to try to be faithful to what you feel."

"How do I do that?"

"By not lying to yourself or others. If you feel sad or angry or scared, accept the truth of that feeling and try to let that feeling guide your actions. Sometimes that means having a deep feeling, sometimes it means talking to people about what you're feeling. And no, you don't lose what you've gained of yourself in one lie or misunderstanding or missed feeling. But since you have a chance to let those lost parts of yourself flourish, do what you can to help them grow. The image that comes to me is one of a garden that, through years of not being taken care of properly, has become so overgrown with weeds that you can't even see the flowers bloom. But then if you consistently work on the garden, if you clear away the weeds, trim the hedges, fertilize, after a while it begins to look like a garden again. After that, if you miss doing things for a few weeks, the garden doesn't immediately look wild and uncared for, but if you neglect it for months and years it goes back to the original state. The same thing holds true for what I like to think of as your internal garden. Work steadily on it and changes begin to take place; neglect it and it can, over time, revert to wilderness. And once you have a garden in shape you don't have to do major work on it constantly, every day—just periodically. That's what can happen with you and your feelings, too."

"Okay, that makes me feel better. I didn't like the

idea that not feeling was like committing a mortal sin, and all your work is wiped out immediately."

"No, it doesn't quite work like that with feelings. You make mistakes, but you can learn and grow from them."

"I'm suddenly starting to worry that I won't know what to do with my feelings now that I don't get to see you every day. Can you give me some pointers?"

I thought for a moment and then said, "One thing to remember is that the intensive *is* so intense simply because you are focusing on your feelings every day. When you enter your regular life of school or work that all changes—and rightly so. This intensive is meant to help you become aware of and sensitive to your feelings and teach you, as well, how to go into them when you need to. Having deep feelings is not meant to be the focus of your life. The ability to feel and resolve your pain when you need to is meant to help you live your life more fully—with greater awareness and, hopefully, happiness. Having feelings is a means to an end, not the end itself.

"Having said that, I will also say that it helps if you let yourself be sensitive to your feelings, to be aware of them rather than ignoring or denying them. Sometimes what you feel can be very dramatic and intense and internally clear. You *know* that you are angry or sad. But at other times it can be very subtle, just a very quiet inner voice or a slight twinge of emotion that you feel. Most of us have spent so much time denying our feelings that we don't listen to that voice. Or sometimes we've been taught that our inner voice doesn't matter, that other people's needs and wishes are what count. This isn't true. The truth is that *our* feelings matter, as well as others'. It can take a long time to feel the real balance between others' needs and your own, others' feelings and yours, but one of the first steps is hearing yours.

"The other point I would like to mention is keeping your balance. When you are a person who has been raised to believe that others' needs and wishes are more to be considered than your own and then in therapy you discover that what you need and want actually does matter, it is very easy to go to the other extreme, the one I call the 'entitlement of the deprived.' In that state it seems only fitting that now only *your* needs count, especially if you have spent most of your life giving too much. You can feel that since you've given so much, you are entitled to get more than your fair share now. So be on the lookout for that attitude in yourself as well." I suddenly noticed how very much *I* had been talking. This was the talk I usually saved for the *end* of the last session, to prepare the patient for group therapy and working with other therapists. I decided it was time for me to be quiet and try to listen for what my patient was feeling.

"Does that mean that people who have always tried to get more than their fair share suddenly have a tendency to be overgenerous?" she asked.

That made me laugh. "Unfortunately, no. People

who come into therapy with that problem usually have to work long and hard to change it."

SILENCE

My patient suddenly got very agitated—tossing, turning, and twisting a bit of tissue in her hands. "What happens if I need to talk to you? Or if I have a really big feeling and I don't know what to do? What if I have a big problem?"

"You know, I'll be happy to answer those questions because they are relevant, but I have a feeling that there's more going on than you needing the logical answers."

SILENCE

Her agitation increased. She sighed several times.

SILENCE

"Do you think you can tell me what's going on?" I was really wondering. Did it have to do with her question about being too giving? Was she anxious that we were near the end of her intensive? I didn't have a clue.

"No, I'm not too sure." She had a sullen sound to her voice and she stared at the ceiling.

"Really?" My voice had a questioning lilt. I was sure she had some idea.

"I feel all confused."

"Tell me about it." Maybe I could get a clearer idea of what was bothering her by asking more directly.

"I don't know what to say."

"Take some time and let yourself notice what's going on inside." She gave a sharp twitch to the blanket she was wrapped in, giving a sigh at the same time.

SILENCE

The silence seemed to drag on forever. What was going on inside her head? "I get the feeling you don't want to talk."

She kept her silence, but gave the blanket a flutter kick.

SILENCE

She just kept lying there, not saying one word. I was starting to get uncomfortable myself. This was a definite impasse. I ran over all the things we had talked about up to this point. She really had questioned me about being on her own. Maybe it was end-of-intensive anxiety. "How are you feeling about this being the very last session of your intensive?"

"Why do you ask me that?" she questioned suspiciously.

"I'm just wondering."

"I'm not happy about it." She rolled over on her side, turning her back to me.

"You seem pretty upset."

"Well, I'm not."

"Seems that way to me."

"I don't want to talk."

SILENCE

Now what should I do? She was definitely on strike and was refusing to tell me anything. How could I do therapy through that? I had some time to think about it all, since she wanted to be quiet. Was there anything I could say to break the impasse? Nothing occurred to me. So I decided that since I had nothing to say, I should stay quiet. I knew she was avoiding telling me something, but I didn't want to *force* it out of her. I knew I *could* force her to talk, but that seemed much too much like all the other forced situations of her life. I didn't want the end of her intensive therapy with me to be another trauma.

SILENCE . . . LONG SILENCE

"If you don't want to talk because there is something going on inside you that you need to think out on your own, that's fine. But if, as I suspect, you are being so quiet because there is something that is hard for you to talk about, you are doing yourself a disservice. Our time is limited and you would do well to use it well." I thought that would give her something to think about. I continued, "Please check what is happening inside you and see if this is a helpful silence that you need or one that is destructive to your goals in therapy."

I was hoping that my comments would help her get a clearer sense of what she was doing. Meanwhile, I was in deep thought. What had happened? I went back over the session in my mind. We had talked about what she learned during the intensive, about what would happen if she wasn't always one hundred percent true to herself—an impossibility if I'd ever heard one. What had happened next? She had started to ask me about what would happen if she needed to talk to me. How had I replied? For some reason, I was blocking. I couldn't really remember what I had said. That was a big clue. In general, I have an excellent memory for conversation, so why wasn't I remembering it now? Obviously, I'd done something wrong. Once I admitted that to myself, my memory cleared. I'd faded out for a moment and asked her the wrong kind of question. I had answered the words she'd been saying, but not the deeper feeling. She was afraid, but I hadn't been listening closely enough. I was quiet for quite a while, waiting to see if she wanted to initiate, then spoke. "What's going on?"

"I don't know; I feel all upset and confused, but I really, really don't know what it is."

"I think what happened was that I made a mistake. It got really sticky after you asked me what if . . . you needed to talk to me, you had a big feeling. That's where it went wrong. I think I heard the words, but not what you were really asking me. So let's go right back there. Can you remember how you felt when I said I thought there was something more going on, that I would answer your questions later?"

SILENCE

"I felt really bad. Like I'd done the wrong thing."

"I'm sorry. . . . Can you tell me what the worst of it was?"

There was a long pause.

"I was asking you for something. I was leaning toward you, in a feeling way, and it felt like you pushed me back."

I felt bad now, because that in fact was what I had done, by not hearing her. It was important to validate the truth. "You're right. How are you feeling this very moment?"

"I feel angry and sad."

"What do you want to tell me?"

"You hurt my feelings. You made me feel really bad. You didn't understand me."

"That's right, I didn't. What did that do to you?"

"I suddenly felt all, all alone. Like you were here, but you weren't." She looked totally miserable, rolled up in a ball. "There never is anyone there when I need them. I have to do everything on my own. Nobody ever helps me."

What about what I'm doing right now? went winging through my head, though I didn't say that, since in the context of her feeling what I was doing now was totally irrelevant. Trying to help her now didn't change her feeling of a few minutes ago one bit. "That is a very familiar feeling, isn't it?"

"It seems to always be with me."

"That feeling of being all alone?"

"It haunts me like a ghost."

She sounded sad, but far from being able to feel. I was also wondering about that anger she felt. I knew it was hard for her to express anger and also knew it could be very difficult for her to express it to me. "So what does it do to you when someone pushes you into that feeling, by what they say or do?"

"I already told you that." She sounded peeved.

"Yeah." I said this in a totally deadpan voice. If I got all warm and comforting now she would eventually cry and feel the sadness, but would miss the opportunity to feel her anger with me. I knew if she could feel the anger, she would also get to the sadness.

"What did you tell me?"

"That it made me sad."

"You said more than that."

"Yeah." Now she was imitating me. It was working. She was getting closer to the anger.

"Say what you're feeling."

"You're trying to make me angry."

"You already are angry. Why don't you let yourself say it?"

"I'm angry." This in a completely lifeless voice.

"Is that how you feel it?"

"No."

"So tell me exactly the way you feel it."

"I'm angry." Still very little expression showed in her voice.

"Come on, there's more there. I know it."

"I'm angry at you." She spit it out in a low, intense voice, clipping her words.

"Go on, there's more. Let every bit of it out."

"I'm angry. You left me all alone."

SILENCE

"That's right, I did. Tell me what you think of that."

"I hate it. No one *ever* stays with me. I have to do

127

all the hard things by myself." She was sounding angry, but still very restrained. I thought to myself, This has to do with today being the last day as well. It isn't just what I said that has made her angry.

"All by yourself?"

"That's right. Now the intensive is over, and I'll be all alone to do this by myself. I'll be all alone." She fell silent.

I let the silence go on, then asked, "What else?"

"I suddenly feel too tired to say anything. It's too hard."

Didn't I know that feeling myself? Especially when you think you're not supposed to be getting angry at all. "Too tired?"

"It doesn't do any good anyway."

"You still sound upset."

"What difference does it make? Nothing changes."

"What do you need to change?"

"I need someone to stay with me."

"Say that to *me*." I knew she needed to start with me, though I didn't know exactly where it would end up in her past. I also knew that if I directed her into her past too quickly, she would miss her opportunity to be openly angry with someone in authority and live to tell the tale. Besides feeling in the past, she needed chances to do things differently *now*. This was as good a place to start as any and better than most, in that I would let her have her say, without defending myself.

"I need you to stay with me, not run off, like everybody else does. I felt more alone when you asked me that stupid question than when you really leave the room. I need someone to be with me. I'm tired of being left alone to do everything myself." She was speaking in a low, intense voice. She mostly looked at the floor, but she occasionally fixed me with a piercing glance.

"Go on."

"I'm always being left alone to do everything by myself, *all* by myself." She raised her voice on "all."

"Use your body."

She started slapping her hand down by her side. "This is the way it always *(slap!)* is. No one *(slap!)* is *ever (slap!)* there when I *(slap!)* need them. No one is ever there when I am afraid! I'm always stealing when I try to get what I need!"

Lyrics from The Band's song flashed incredibly quickly through my mind. "Tears of rage, tears of grief / Why must I always be the thief?"

She hurled herself into a ball in the corner—tense, still, and silent. "Let yourself go on," I encouraged.

"It doesn't do any good." She sounded tired and worn.

"You sound so tired."

"I feel tired. My body, my heart, my soul all feel too tired to go on. There's just too much for me to have to do."

"When you shouted before, it made me think of a song by that group The Band. Do you know them?"

"Yes, I've heard them before."

"Tears of rage, tears of grief, / Why must I always be the thief?" I sang.

SILENCE

I saw a slight relaxation of her body. "How are you a thief?" I asked.

"You remember my feeling when I hugged my mother."

"Yes, I do." A feeling of sadness flowed through me.

"Well, it's the same thing here. I felt I was asking too many questions, wanting too much from you."

"And then what did you feel?"

"That I didn't want to say anything, because I never know when it's too much until my feelings are already hurt."

"Didn't you feel angry, too?"

"Yes, I did. But I'm not supposed to be angry."

"What made you angry?"

"You tricked me."

"How did I do that?" I was surprised here. But I knew this wasn't the time to try to explain what I thought I'd been doing with her.

"You made me think it was okay to need something from you, then you didn't like it when I did."

"What did I do that made you feel that?" I was acutely aware that if I tried to be ambiguous and imply that her perception was in any way incorrect or that I disagreed I would only serve to close her off again.

"You wouldn't answer my question."

"Even more than that, I didn't really hear what you were asking, did I?"

"No, you didn't."

"What were you really saying to me when you asked all those questions?"

"I was telling you that I was scared." Her voice trembled a bit there.

"Yes?" I said.

"I am scared. I'm scared I'm going to be all alone with my feelings without you to help me anymore."

SILENCE

"And what else do you need to tell me?" I asked this very quietly and gently.

"Don't leave me. Please don't leave me all alone." She looked up at me with tears in her eyes. I couldn't tell her that I wouldn't leave her because of course, in a certain sense, I would. I wouldn't be available to her on a daily basis as I had been during the intensive. But I couldn't say that to her at this moment of supreme vulnerability, especially after my inadvertent rebuff earlier in the session. I simply stretched out my hand, putting it very close to hers. She clasped it tightly, pulling it close, then started crying deep and hard. I was touched and saddened. It made me wish for a magic wand, so I could take her pain—and everyone else's—away. But I knew that I couldn't do that either. The only choice I truly had was to help her feel this as deeply as she could so she could heal. I slowly drew my hand away as she went deeper into her crying. My mind traveled slowly over the events of her life as I wondered where this feeling would lead. Then I recalled events in my own life that had left me with a similar deep "well of loneliness."

My thoughts focused on her again as she cried deep, deep sobs and began to speak. "Please. Please. Don't leave me alone. It's too scary for me. What if something really bad happens and I don't know what to do? Who can I turn to? There isn't anyone." As she cried more and more deeply, it was soon obvious that she wasn't talking to me anymore as she carried on with her tears. She had turned onto her back and she had a pillow pressed to her stomach; every now and again she would wave her hand in the air and say "good-bye," then cry even more deeply. Her cries were not very loud, but they were incredibly intense. I could feel that she was holding nothing back. She wasn't thinking of me or what I thought or how she looked or sounded; every fiber of her being was fully concentrated around the pain she was feeling. Then there was a shift. She began to say, "It's not fair, it's really not fair, you are never here when I need you." Now she sounded angry and she started slapping her hand down on the mat again. "*Never, ever* when I need you. Then I have to be understanding. I hate understanding. I wish I were stupid, then I wouldn't have to understand. I don't want to understand! I don't want to understand!" Shouting this over and over, she shook her fist in the air, then started pounding on the foam-covered wall. "I don't care, I don't care why. I want you here *now*."

Still holding the pillow, she slid onto her stomach and began sobbing and crying, pounding her legs up and down and thrashing like a very young child. She kept crying for a long time without any words. Then she started speaking again: "I want my mommy I don't want you. Go away. I want my mommy now. I want my mommy. No!" She bolted up into a kneeling position, grabbed the edge of the padding on the wall, and began shaking it back and forth. "I want Mommy. Mommy. Mommy. Mommy." Then she backed up, waving her right hand back and forth and pushing something away. Next she stopped, looked into her empty palm, and made a flinging gesture. "I don't want that, I want my mommy," she shouted, and falling down onto the mat full-length, she sobbed and cried over and over, "I want my mommy."

I knew she was in a deep feeling and that it was about her mother—and also that it had been precipitated by my mistake earlier in the session—but other than that I had no idea where she was going. I had a strong sense of trust in the process, as well as clear indicators that she was actually in the throes of a connected incident in her past. Based on my experiences in working with other people and my own personal feeling work, I was confident that she was on the right track, and I had no impulse to interrupt the process in order to get a clearer understanding. I knew she would tell me later. With another patient in a different set of circumstances, interrupting and asking questions might be exactly the right thing to help her get clear what was happening, but this was not necessary now. My only function at this point was to be a quiet witness.

I stayed alert, watching all she was doing so I could be a help to her in the clarification process later. She cried steadily for a good fifteen or twenty minutes; then her crying began to slow down, becoming quieter and less intense. Soon she was lying quietly on her back, still holding the pillow to her chest; occasionally she gave it a little pat. She must have stayed there for a full ten minutes without a word. Then she reached out and took a wad of tissue and gave a honking blow of her nose. I gave a little chuckle, thinking, First things first.

"Whew! I certainly went on a time journey there," she said in a quiet, low voice.

"It surely looked like it from here," I confirmed.

"It was two different times of the same feeling. The first one was at about age twelve and the second one I was two or three. This is really amazing. One just led into the other. Even though the feeling was exactly the same, the time frame was completely different. It all started with you today. I got so upset that you wouldn't answer my question. It was you, but it wasn't only you. Even while it was happening I was wondering why I was *so* upset, but I couldn't really see it. It somehow felt that I was wrong or, failing that, you were wrong. Now I can see it so clearly."

"What do you see?"

"I see that my feeling with you was so strong because of the feeling of the past."

"What happened as you were feeling?"

"Well, the first time was during a time that my father was stationed in another state by the military. He was away for about one year altogether. He came to visit us twice during that time, I think. On one of those visits my mother got pregnant. While he was away, we got the military family allotment, which wasn't enough to support my mother and eight children. He sent her only eighteen dollars during that year, so she had to work. She found a position as a psychiatric attendant in a state mental hospital, and she worked the night shift, which was from eleven at night to seven in the morning. The job paid more for work at night, and she wanted to be at home when we left for school and when we came home.

"The scene I remembered was as she was leaving for work on a really cold snowy night. She was about six or seven months pregnant, so she was really sticking out there. I was left in charge when she left. I was twelve, my next brother was ten, the first set of twins were nine, my next sister was seven, the brother after her was five, and the second set of twins were three. It was very frightening to me that I was the oldest person there, with so many little children in my charge. I would worry about there being a fire or one of them getting dangerously ill. I had my mother's number at work, but she was about a twenty-minute drive away.

So sometimes I would try to talk to her about how frightened I was. She wouldn't really let me. She would shut me up by saying that she had to go to work, which I knew was true; if she didn't, there wouldn't be enough food for all of us. Then she would ask me if I thought she really wanted to work, as tired as she was and as pregnant as she was. Of course I knew the answer was no. And finally she would say that I just had to understand that as much as she didn't want to go, she had to and that I had to be the one in charge because I was the oldest and there was no one else who could do it. Then she would look at me really directly and fiercely and say, 'Do you understand?' All I could do was nod my head yes." Here she began to cry again.

"It makes me so sad for both of us because I knew she was scared, too. She needed for me to be strong so she could go to work, so I tried to be. I would act perfectly competent until I saw her get into her car. Then I would lean against the front door and cry about how scared I was. 'Please don't leave me,' I would whisper as I cried. I really wished that I didn't understand, so I could make a big fuss and make her stay home, but I . . . but I knew she couldn't."

She stopped talking, put her face in her hands, and cried and cried. After a while she looked up and said, "I can't really stay mad at her because I do understand, it was just a sad situation. Basically she was a single mother with eight children and pregnant with the ninth, no support from her husband, who was a thousand miles away, and she was thirty-seven years old. The worst part about it all, though, was that it has left me with a really strong feeling that I am not allowed to need anything from anyone. If I do need something I just try to soldier on, and not be a burden. I knew she had too much to handle and I really did want to help her, but I was just too young for all that responsibility."

"It sounds as if you have some more things to say to her," I said.

"Mommy, I'm just too young, I'm not big enough to help you." She cried a little bit longer after saying her piece, rested quietly for a moment, then spoke again.

"It's so sad how it's affected me. You didn't answer one question, and I was sure you didn't want to help me, that I had done the wrong thing by asking, that this whole thing was an awful trick. Now it seems so simple and clear. As I was crying the whole feeling detached from you and attached back to my mother. Then what you had done didn't seem that important. I guess that's what happens when you make the connection. Now it feels like a simple and pretty small misunderstanding, but then it felt like the end of the world. I was even thinking in the back of my mind that maybe I'd move back to my hometown and not come to therapy anymore!"

"That is powerful."

"And do you know what else? The feeling just slipped all by itself into the even earlier time. I didn't do anything to make that happen. Suddenly I was just there."

"What was that about?"

"Once when we were visiting at my great-grandmother's house, my grandmother was there, too. My mother was going out at night in the car. I wanted to come along and she wouldn't let me, even though she was taking my younger brother. He was about six months old, I guess, since I was two. I kept asking if she was going for long, and she said no, that by the time I woke up she would be back. I went to bed and fell asleep. I woke up later, though, and she *wasn't* back. I started calling for her and crying. I felt sad and mad. I was standing in the crib, holding on to the side rail, shaking it and calling out for her. My grandmother came in and tried to comfort me, and I didn't want her. Then she tried giving me a dime. For some reason, even though I couldn't count and didn't understand about money, I really liked and tried to get dimes. I think it was because they were so small and shiny. This time I was outraged. I really remember feeling she was trying to trick me, and I threw the dime on the floor. Years later, that was one of the funny stories they would tell about me, but then and in the feeling it wasn't funny at all." Then she broke into a little laugh, saying, "Though when I think back on it now, seeing myself as a tiny, screaming banshee in a nightgown, throwing money around, it does give me a laugh."

"That is a pretty neat image. You knew exactly

who and what you wanted and you weren't taking any substitutes."

"It's sad to me that over the years I lost that knowledge; but I feel that through therapy I'm on the track of getting it back again." She said this slowly and thoughtfully. "I wish I could just magically undo all the bad things that happened and suddenly feel absolutely wonderful. But I can see that just as it was a slow process of loss that changed me, it will have to be a slow process to change back. It was so slow, so insidious, losing myself. I can't pinpoint one moment when it happened, just that over time I had become someone who didn't dare to know what she thought and felt. I've lost so much time. When I get dramatic I think of it like the title of a movie . . . *The Lost Childhood.* Maybe now I can change the title, through therapy to . . . let's see . . . *The Found Life!* That's how I feel, what was lost is being found." She gave a little self-deprecating laugh. "How's that for drama?"

"Sounds pretty real to me."

She had been tracing little spiral patterns in the carpet with her finger. Now she looked up at me. "One thing I know for sure: I want to be able to say what I want and need. I never really do that now. I'm about to go back to my everyday life. Will I be able to do things differently?"

"That is the work that you need to do. I know I've told you that therapy doesn't make life easy, it just changes the absolutely impossible to the difficult. And when we first begin to work on habits and patterns that have been driven by pain and fear for so many years, it can be extremely difficult. But I can say from personal experience, it can be done. Where there is a will, there is a way."

"That is something else I've gained during this intensive—my will, my feeling that I have the right to work toward something that is important to me. I guess that is pretty good for such a short period of time."

"It absolutely is," was my reply.

After she gathered her things to go, she stood up and stuck out her hand. "I want to tell you now, before I feel too shy. Thank you very much."

I took her hand in both of mine and told her with equal emphasis, "You are welcome. I'll see you in group. And to answer your earlier question, you definitely *may* call me when you need to. Good-bye." I felt a surge of hope and joy. I felt I was sending her off on a great voyage of discovery.

PART II

Deep Feeling Therapy:
An Overview

Primal Therapy

I was originally trained as a Primal therapist, and I also received Primal Therapy as a patient.
Thus, even though I now practice a form of psychotherapy that departs at several points from Primal
Therapy methodology, you may find it helpful to
have an explanation of Primal Therapy before I de-
lineate the differences in my own clinical work,
which I call Deep Feeling Therapy.

Primal Therapy is a form of psychotherapy that
posits that childhood trauma has long-term effects
on the adult personality. It differs from many other
therapies in that its emphasis is on actually *reliving*
the deep, powerful emotional component of the earlier trauma. I believe conventional psychotherapies
can help patients develop awareness of unconscious

processes, work through transference issues, and repair a great deal of the damage done to the psyche. But I do not believe that they can always adequately address the issue of the mind/body split that takes place when a person has suffered a great deal.

Either the person has the memory of the trauma but is split off from the feelings, or the person has little or no memory of traumatic events and is even more split from his or her experience. Because suffering is not only recorded in the mind, but is recorded and held in the body as well, both aspects of the trauma, mind and body, need healing. So from my therapeutic point of view, healing requires multiple components: insight, understanding, working through transference issues, *and* the full body experience of your deepest emotions. When a person's body as well as his or her mind has been traumatized, by beatings, sexual abuse, or neglect, the person's *body* needs to experience and release this trauma to allow the deepest healing to take place. It is through the therapeutic cojoining of all these elements that it is possible to reconnect the mind and the body at the deepest levels.

As a therapist, I have a favorite analogy: If a person is bitten by a poisonous snake it's not enough for her to understand how it happened, what kind of snake it was, what the effects of the poison will be; it's not even enough to have a knowledgeable, caring doctor present. In order for the damaging effects of the poison to cease, something has to be done to the person's body. Either she must take an antidote, or she must attempt to remove the poison. This is how I view the effects of Deep Feeling Therapy/Primal Therapy: as an antidote to the emotional and physical aspects of childhood pain and trauma.

Primal Therapy also differs from other therapies in its structure. The therapy usually commences with an "intensive" period, which lasts three weeks. During the intensive period, patients are instructed to sever all contact with their normal life. They do not work, attend school, smoke, drink, or take drugs. At the discretion of their therapist, they do not watch television, listen to the radio, speak to family or friends on the telephone, read, or do any of the things they normally do to avoid their pain. The purpose of this isolation is twofold. First, it allows patients the leisure time to reflect on and be open to memories and feelings of their childhood. And second, it prevents the usual avoidance of those same memories and feelings by absorption in distracting activities. Most people never spend a moment alone, much less alone with nothing to do. This "alone time" is often quite effective in awakening forgotten memories. While the patient is in this intensive therapy, he or she is seen by the therapist for open-ended sessions five days of the week. "Open ended" means the sessions last from one and a half to two and a half hours as necessary, and on very rare occasions longer than that.

The next phase of the therapy comes at the end

of the intensive period, when the patients begin what is actually the longest and deepest part of the therapy. During this second period they continue the work begun in the intensive, and deeper integration of the insights that have come from feeling begins. I do not mean to imply that it is *simply* by crying or experiencing a deep feeling that one heals. It is in the interaction between several crucial elements that change comes about: deep feeling, insight and integration of those insights, being heard with true interest and personal care, the transference of childhood feelings onto the therapist, and working them through. It is within the crucible of these collected elements that Deep Feeling Therapy does its work.

A Deep Feeling Therapy or Primal Therapy group is different from conventional group therapy in several ways. The group begins in a dimly lit room with people lying on the well-padded, carpeted floor, with their heads resting on pillows. A box of tissues is usually nearby. The most dramatic difference is that these groups begin with a one-on-one meeting between each patient and the therapist or therapists who are conducting the group. It is during this period that the individual patient has the chance to speak privately with the therapist who is working with him or her and to receive help going into whatever his or her feeling is. Each person works individually with a therapist for about fifteen to twenty minutes. Once the patient has gone deeply into the feeling, often crying about what is causing the pain, the therapist leaves him or her and goes on to help someone else. This period usually lasts from one to one and a half hours, depending on the size of the group. When I myself first entered therapy, a group could easily consist of one hundred patients with ten therapists or therapists-in-training circulating around the room and working individually with patients. The noise level could rise incredibly with sometimes as many as seventy-five people crying, sobbing, or shouting at the same time.

The second phase of group therapy is called "post group." During this phase the lights are brightened; patients sit up and have an opportunity to speak about what is troubling them and the insights they might have had, or to confront other patients or therapists with feelings or perceptions they have about them. If a person is not done with the feeling or he begins to cry, he can work with a therapist again. The post group is usually led by one or more senior therapists. Their function is to see that in that highly charged emotional environment, patients are not allowed to reenact their childhood traumas using other patients as the victims; they also identify and help patients bring their feelings to the surface and work them through in the arena of the group.

Many patients find this large-group setting frightening and intimidating. In my experience it was usually the more forceful and outgoing people who received the most benefit from this form of therapy. It was extremely easy for the quieter and more frightened patients to fall through the cracks and to lose their opportunity to grow and heal in this environment, or even to be harmed or retraumatized if they were verbally attacked by one of the more angry, aggressive patients.

I believe that group therapy is a very effective modality, but I have found that in the context of working with someone's deepest and most vulnerable emotions, it is most effective when used in conjunction with continuing individual therapy sessions with the same therapist. Janov's point of view seemed to be that once the patient learned how to open to his or her feelings, individual therapy was no longer truly necessary. I use group therapy in my practice but over the years have found that a small-group format consisting of eight to ten patients, that offers the consistency of working with the same therapist or therapists on a regular basis, to be most helpful.

Deep Feeling Therapy

I SHOULD POINT OUT THAT THE THERAPY I USE in my practice, though based on and using many Primal Therapy techniques, is different in many aspects from Primal Therapy as I was originally taught it. To prevent confusion I call my work Deep Feeling Therapy. My work is based on the actual needs of the patient, as I perceive them, in a given therapy session and over the long term of therapy, instead of strictly adhering to Janov's methodology.

The major points of divergence between Deep Feeling Therapy and Primal Therapy as I was originally trained to practice it are in offering long-term individual therapy following the three-week intensive, and on the issues of the transference and homosexuality.

At times Primal Therapy methodology has been at odds with the needs of the patient; in that case, for me, the needs of the patient must take precedence. Over the years, many of my assumptions and beliefs have been challenged and changed by the patients with whom I have worked. One of the most profound was concerning homosexuality. In my early training I was taught that homosexuality was neurosis based on a need for one's same sex parent and that one of the goals of therapy should be a change in the person's sexual orientation. I had some doubts about that point of view, but continued to work from that perspective for many years, until one of my male patients questioned his place in a therapy that held everything he was to be anathema. Through his courage and honesty I was led to question that assumption deeply. At this point, I feel that although both the heterosexual and homosexual orientation can have their neurotic acting-out aspects, a homosexual orientation in and of itself is not evidence of neurosis necessitating a cure.

In my current work I employ the three-week intensive because I have found that it is an invaluable learning and growth opportunity for both patient and therapist. I have experimented a few times with beginning the therapy without an intensive but have found that it doesn't work well over the long term; in some cases a shorter intensive has been effective, but my experience is that when the intensive is omitted it takes much longer for patients to allow themselves to begin to open up to deep feelings. I have also found that without the feeling of safety that comes from patients knowing they will see the therapist the very next day after an intense or frightening session, strong resistance and defensive behaviors can arise.

I continue to hold open-ended sessions during the initial three weeks because it is in the freedom from pressing time constraints that patients can allow themselves to open more freely to the deepest emotions—especially in the early phase of therapy, when patients are learning to trust the therapist, themselves, and the process of the therapy.

It is after the intensive that Deep Feeling Therapy and Primal Therapy part company. One innovation that I began during my private practice in New York and have found to be essential is continuing weekly individual sessions. In the early days of Primal Therapy, once the intensive phase of therapy was complete, patients could usually only see their intensive therapist in group sessions, and then often irregularly. On many occasions patients would not have the opportunity to work with their original therapist but would be assigned to work with someone else. The reasoning behind this was based on Janov's original contention that transference—the tendency to transfer to others feelings and attitudes that were originally associated with important figures in early childhood, particularly parents—was not a factor in Primal Therapy. Continuing this line of reasoning, it shouldn't matter. Any therapist could work with a patient as long as he or she could help the patient discover and feel her feelings. This is a point with which I most strongly disagree. I believe that it is in the context of a long-term, committed relationship between therapist and patient that the most growth and healing can take place. The original Primal Therapy method is excellent in bringing about healing between the patient and his feelings. But it does very little to address, over the long term, how the person reacts and interacts over time in an intimate, long-term relationship. How could this be addressed when the therapeutic relationship itself is very focused and intimate during the three-week intensive period, but is then abruptly terminated when the patient enters group therapy, becomes one of many patients, and only periodically has the opportunity to work with the original therapist?

I remember remarking to my fellow trainees during my early training that it seemed to me that the *therapists* in the training program seemed to get much greater benefit from the therapy than the patients did. I now believe that this was due to the continuity that was achieved in the training program. During our training, in our training groups, and in our individual therapy, we had the opportunity to work with the same therapists over and over; it was under these circumstances that most of my deepest and most intense healing experiences took place.

When I began my private practice, I decided to test the accuracy of my perceptions regarding the efficacy of seeing the same therapist again and again as opposed to having an occasional session here and there with different therapists. At that time I was working with a partner as well as conducting a small therapists-training program. We began to allow and encourage our patients to schedule weekly individual sessions. In a very short time I began to see an increase in the depth of the work that was possible, and over the long term, a change in the patients' ability to operate with a greater and more consistent level of honesty, trust, and awareness in the therapeutic relationship. With time this ability carried over into the conduct of the patient's everyday life and brought about significant improvement of not just her inner life, but her ability to function comfortably in intimate relationships and productively in her chosen field.

It was while working with individual patients in a weekly therapeutic setting that I discovered that the transference was very much alive and well. This discovery process began while I was still a trainee therapist and was often assigned to work with patients whose original therapist was no longer available to work with them. Many of these patients had strong feelings of loss and abandonment that they brought up when they entered group therapy. They very frequently related these feelings to the original parental relationship and struggled mightily to reestablish the relationship they had had with their original intensive therapist, using the same behaviors they had used to try to get attention from their parents. At that time, Institute patients who tried to insist on working with their original therapist were labeled as "acting out" symbolically, and they were strongly urged to get over those feelings. I had read a great deal of the works of Sigmund Freud and it was clear to me that what I was witnessing was a transference phenomenon. How could it be anything else, since we all transfer childhood experience to our present-day life in or out of therapy? In later years this awareness of transference issues became the basis of my difference from Primal Therapy.

It seems to me that transference will inevitably occur in the intensity of any meaningful therapeutic relationship, since it is often the most intimate relationship the person has ever had, requiring a level of honesty and vulnerability that many of us have never previously experienced. So it naturally follows that many powerful childhood feelings will arise in the context of this therapeutic relationship and be directed at one's therapist. The result is the reactivation of the dynamic of the original parental relationships. The patient begins to relate to the therapist based on what she experienced as a child. The difference is that in the context of therapy there is no repetition of the previous traumatic experience. When there is an event that is similar to the original pain—for example, the therapist goes on vacation or is ill, thus abandoning the patient, or misses the mark in a therapeutic intervention—the patient has the opportunity to talk about it and the chance to feel it, and has support in following these feelings back to their root in the parental relationship. And over time, by this continued examination and experiencing of feelings, he begins to understand and develop beyond these childhood responses. What better place to have these feelings come up and be worked through than in a situation where one's feelings, fears, rages, and vulnerabilities are taken seriously and allowed free expression, with the opportunity to follow them back to the root cause and resolve them? This is what happens in Deep Feeling Therapy.

I do not want to imply that in classical Primal Therapy there is no transference. I know that there is. My point is that without the safety of a consistent therapeutic relationship, these transference and countertransference issues are not adequately addressed. From my years in private practice of Deep Feeling Therapy I see very clearly the benefit of having the opportunity to do this very fruitful individual work.

General Parameters
of Treatment

THOUGH I THINK THAT MANY OF THE VALUES I
place on "good therapy" are implicit in the body of
this book, I would like to express them explicitly
here. First, a definition of Deep Feeling/Primal is
necessary. For me these terms mean a connected total descent into the emotional reality of a past traumatic event. This means the patient returns, in the
feeling, to the moment of trauma and experiences
the emotion of that time. By "connected" I mean
there is a definite awareness of what the past trauma
was and, as well, a clear sense of the activating event
in the present, if there is one. Often this clarity arises
after the beginning of the feeling process, but in
order for the deepest healing to take place, understanding is necessary. It is not enough that a person
cries or rages about something in the past or present
with a vague sense that he is unhappy or angry,
though many deep feelings begin in a state of such
confusion. With deeper access to the levels of the
feeling, understanding does come.

I want to make it clear that it is not the position
of the therapist to badger or demand that some-

one understand what is happening to him. With good support from the therapist, a person in pain will naturally, over time, clearly see and feel what happened to him, and develop insights about the long-term effects of the early trauma. He will also develop the ability to change the behaviors driven by those past traumas. It is not easy work, but it is possible.

This is a natural healing process and just as a person's body does not need instructions to heal a broken bone (though a cast may be necessary to support the healing), the psyche works toward health with the support of appropriate therapy. Appropriate therapy is based on the patient's needs, not those of the therapist. Therapists who need to think of themselves as "great therapists" will find it difficult to allow the patient the time and space necessary to progress at her own pace; by the same token, a therapist with a need to be a "good guy" might find it extremely difficult to confront a client about self-destructive or acting-out behaviors. For these reasons I find it is absolutely essential that the therapist be far along in his or her own feeling progression before attempting to be of help to others. As a therapist you cannot follow, much less lead, someone into emotional terrain you have not journeyed through yourself.

Trustworthiness is a sine qua non in this work, and it is attained by having made the journey. It would be foolish to accept as the leader for a climb up Mt. Everest someone who has only hiked through the easy trails of a well-marked city park, and the same is true of forays into the depths of childhood emotional pain. When a therapist *has* done the prerequisite work on herself, it can be easier to avoid certain insensitivities, such as asking the patient if she is sure events took place as she has stated, or making excuses for the parents, or pressuring the client to be forgiving and understanding of the parents' problems. Forgiveness is a state that comes on its own—if it comes—and cannot be mandated by a therapist. Further, it can be frightening, and rightfully so in some instances, to both therapist and patient to traverse some particularly horrific emotional territory. When the therapist has experienced and worked through her own places of this nature, she can be appropriately encouraging, when necessary, as well as aware of times when the patient needs help in stopping a feeling that is too overwhelming. If, on the other hand, the therapist is one who has not tackled her own demons, she can easily push a patient into areas he or she is not yet strong enough to feel in an integrated way. Or she may not be able to help a patient exit from a feeling too intense to be felt at that time. In other words: this form of therapy is strong medicine, to be administered only by those who have experienced its effects themselves.

The balance of power in a Deep Feeling session is a delicate matter. Often people seeking help in this form of therapy have been repeatedly traumatized by having their emotional and physical boundaries breached against their will. So when resistance arises, as it will, the therapist must walk a thin line between encouraging the patient to venture into areas of feeling and memory that are difficult, and pushing him where he may not be ready to go. One of the ways to handle this is to encourage the person to make the attempt, rather than to order him to do so. Better to view oneself as a coach offering support than as a boss telling what must be done. I also keep in mind how I myself felt in those difficult spots and what was helpful to me. It is a therapist's job to encourage a patient's growth and to aid in the development of his or her own power, rather than to become another false repository of the power that is rightfully the patient's.

Who Is a Candidate for Deep Feeling Therapy?

ENTERING THIS KIND OF THERAPY REQUIRES AN enormous commitment on the part of the patient. It requires just as much of a commitment from the therapist. This process demands courage, trust, patience, and a long-term commitment from both parties. I am not of the school of Primal therapists who think that everyone on the face of the earth should enter this therapy. Taking a step of this magnitude must be freely done and based on each person's sense of what he or she feels and thinks will be most helpful. I believe that most people could benefit from a deeper awareness and connection to their emotions, but also recognize that not everyone has the desire or the inner resources to do this kind of work. I find that the people who are the most successful in utilizing this therapy method have a strong, intense desire to work on their feelings. They usually enter the therapy from one or the other of two extremes. From one direction comes the person who has a clear awareness that his feelings are powerfully painful and often inappropriate for a given situation (e.g., the person who is devastated or enraged at the smallest criticism or who finds himself unable to utilize talents and capabilities that he clearly possesses). From the other end of the spectrum comes the person who has a sense that he has lost the ability to experience emotion. These people usually enter therapy after some event that brings this loss clearly into awareness; for example, when a beloved relative dies, this person may be unable to cry or feel saddened.

I have not found that this therapy is any more or less helpful to people of any one gender. Both men and women can benefit from the ability to feel and resolve a painful childhood. The difference I often see, however, is the direction from which it is easiest for men and women to approach their pain. In the early stages of therapy men seem to have more difficulty in accessing feelings of sadness and vulnerability, finding greater ease in admitting feelings of anger and rage. Women, on the other hand, often have no difficulty at all in crying or feeling sadness, while attempting to repress and deny anger and rage. Of course, this is a generalization and is not true in all cases.

I believe this difference has nothing to do with a gender-based ability to experience emotion but everything to do with socialization. Boys are taught from the earliest ages that tears are for sissies and babies and are ridiculed and shamed when they release their pain by crying; at the same time, girls are trained to "be nice," to placate others' rage and to deny their own. Though they are allowed the luxury of tears, they, too, can be treated contemptuously for crying. During the course of therapy both men and women gain access to both areas of feeling.

As to the gender or race of the therapist and any effect on the course of therapy, it naturally has an impact, but in my experience, this is an intrapsychic matter, and the effect differs with each person and only becomes clear as therapy progresses.

Technical Aspects

Up to this point I have written about the general format of Deep Feeling Therapy, but now I would like to talk about the specifics of what happens in an individual session. There are several technical concepts that I will introduce in this section. These techniques are: *the opening; setting the scene; following the line of pain; the use of voice;* and *silence.* These concepts all have specific meanings in the context of helping the patient actually enter the moment of trauma and "feel the feeling," so I will define them as they arise.

It is the basic premise of this form of therapy that the healing process requires the patient to feel repressed and denied feelings. I have been asked many times over the years how I "get" someone to feel in a therapy session. I often say jokingly that I do not dance on the patient's chest wearing football cleats. But there is a general pattern that is followed in most feeling therapy sessions, especially in the beginning, when the patient is just learning how to open herself to the deeper levels of her pain. It is the focus of a Deep Feeling therapy session to find the pain in a patient's life and to help her experience it, thereby releasing her from being forced to carry that pain around with her in daily life. Most people who choose this form of therapy have a great deal of sorrow, sadness, and rage that they are aware of on a daily basis. They often experience themselves as in emotional pain, angry, and frightened as they try to control and hide the emotions they experience. There are also people who choose this form of therapy because they experience themselves as emotionally dead and numb. These people also expend a great deal of energy trying to conceal what they don't feel.

A therapy session begins with the patient entering a soundproof room. The walls are usually anywhere from five to ten inches thick so that when the patient begins to cry or rage he can be sure he will not be heard by anyone except the therapist. The room usually has solid-core wooden double doors, with sound-absorbing foam and a vacuum chamber between them. The lights of the room are on a dimmer switch so that they can be lowered to a comfortable, nondistracting level, though some people like the room to be in complete darkness. Just as in the room used for group therapy, there are comfortable upholstered Japanese futon mattresses, soft pillows, cushions, and warm blankets.

As a therapist, I generally sit behind the patient with whom I am working, on a separate set of cushions. The patient can easily have eye contact with me by turning his head. The session begins with the patient telling me how he is. We usually move forward from general social chitchat immediately. It is usually at this point that I ask the patient to "check" or "scan" his body for feelings. By this I mean for the patient to pay close attention to his bodily state; to notice and report any feeling of tension, pain, tightness, or discomfort. The body signals emotional states such as sadness, fright, and anger, as well as physical states such as hunger or sleepiness, by physical sensation. Many patients enter therapy completely disconnected from their bodies and unaware of the integral connection between certain physical sensations and their own emotional state. Once the patient learns to be attuned and responsive to his body's language, the process of opening to feelings becomes much less frightening and mysterious. Patients often report sadness as a sensation of heaviness or pressure in the chest and around the heart; others have a sensation of pressure in the eyes or throat. Anger is sometimes experienced as heat, burning, or tightness in the stomach, chest, or back. Each patient has an individual and unique medley of bodily signals of his or her emotional state. These physical sensations are often the first clue to what the patient is experiencing.

I listen closely and carefully to hear the patient's reported emotional and physical state and endeavor to be aware of any *opening*—a place where the patient's emotional pain about an event he may be describing to me breaks through. An opening can be indicated by a break in the person's voice, a change in the tempo or range of the voice, body language, a change in the breathing rate, or by sighing. When this happens, and it nearly always does, I point it out to the patient and ask him to tell me what he experienced in that moment. Though often a surprise to the person, there is an intensification of emotion around a certain memory or moment in what he was recounting. Most of us have been trained from early childhood *not* to pay attention to what we experience internally, especially if it is a painful feeling, or if we do experience it, not to share awareness of that state but to conceal it.

Once it has been established that there is some pain rising to the surface, we *follow the line of pain.* The patient tries to track the painful emotion from whatever is setting it off in the present, to fully experience the present feeling, then tries to follow this emotion to its origin in his or her past. Sometimes this means all the way back to his earliest childhood memories; at other times it may be as recent as an event in high school or a few years ago.

The next step is *setting the scene*—where the person tries to recall as many pertinent details of that past event as possible. The type of intervention that I would use at this juncture is "to let yourself go back to the moment." I do this because feelings are locked in the specifics of a memory. It is not enough that the patient recalls that she was lonely as a child. If she is going to go back and actually experience being a lonely child, we need to find particular moments.

For one person it might be that she was lonely as she stood with her face pressed to the glass watching hour after hour for her mother to return home from work. For another person it might be the moment when the bedroom door was closed at night and all the light was cut off. For still another, the moment that encapsulates the pain of loneliness might be when she was the only one not chosen when sides were being picked for a ball game.

Once we find the moment, the focus is in talking *into* the feeling rather than using words to avoid the emotional state that is coming up. It is often at this point that a patient's defenses will activate most intensely, because even though he has sought this moment of opportunity to feel in a deep and intense way the past events that are causing him continuing and chronic problems in the present, every aspect of how he usually conducts his life is geared to avoiding feeling. It is often at this moment that the patient wants to begin a theoretical discussion about therapy, or remembers a funny story about his childhood that must be told now, or suddenly forgets what he was talking about. It is at this time that it is most essential that the therapist continue to follow the line of pain and help the patient stay in contact with what he is feeling.

A therapist who has worked on and resolved many of his or her own deepest feelings will have a visceral, as well as an intellectual and emotional awareness of what the patient is suffering in those moments and will therefore be better able to disarm and point out the defenses. By point out I do not mean that the therapist is accusatory and aggressively confrontational, but rather gently and firmly insistent—*suaviter in modo, fortiter in re.* Often just by becoming aware the patient can make the decision to take the plunge and confront the emotional reality in the moment. Therefore it is usually most helpful if the therapist works from a stance that is compassionate and aware, remembering fully how often he himself tried to avoid and deny his own feelings at the beginning of this therapeutic work.

In *setting the scene* all the details count. I try to help the patient with whom I am working remember the time of day, the place, the season of the year, what she and others were wearing, any particular smells, and all other sensory details that can help develop the fully realized return to the patient's past that we are seeking. The feeling can be locked in any of these details.

Let me offer an example. I once worked with a person whose mother came from a family with a history of a serious genetic illness. It usually struck in the early twenties. When my patient's mother had reached her thirties without experiencing any symptoms, she thought she had been spared and decided that it was safe to have children. She had twins. When these children were in the first grade, the mother fell ill. The children went to school one day and when they returned their mother was gone.

She was hospitalized, no longer able to recognize her children or her husband. The children never saw their mother again. She died several years after she was hospitalized.

In our work together my patient maintained that the disappearance of his mother had little effect on him and his brother because they were so well taken care of by their father and grandmother. In recounting this story I had my patient tell me every detail of the moment that their father told them that they wouldn't be seeing their mother again. I had him locate himself in space and time; I helped him recall the weather, the upholstery pattern of the sofa they sat on, even the smell of cooking that permeated the house. My patient had been looking at the foot of the coffee table as his father told the boys that they wouldn't be seeing their mother again, and his further memory of the event was that neither he nor his sibling was too upset.

But as he told the story this time he focused in on the tiniest details, remembering the swirling pattern of the grain of the wood, the way the carpet felt as he rubbed his bare feet back and forth, noticing that he couldn't look at his father, but kept returning his gaze again and again to the round foot of the coffee table. I was very aware during this recounting that my patient became more and more agitated, wringing his hands and breathing faster and faster. Suddenly he gasped and tears began rolling down his face. He started out slowly, gasping several times, trying to stop crying. I encouraged him to let it out, telling him he had held it inside for far too long. Then he began letting out deep, low sobs. He cried for about ten minutes. After blowing his nose and lying there in silence for a few minutes, he told me what had happened. He had suddenly realized that in the memory, the foot of the coffee table was blurry, which let him know that he had cried! This was the beginning of his mourning the loss of his mother.

It should be said that I don't seek details for the sake of details, only in the service of helping to recall the feeling state of an event. So if I have someone who is open to a feeling, already crying or very close to it, I don't interrupt his or her feeling state by asking for unnecessary detail.

The next two concepts I would like to elucidate are *voice* and *silence*. The major point that I would like to make about the voice is that it, too, can be a tool in helping someone descend into the deeper, often darker, realms of feeling. When a patient is speaking about an event that was originally painful to her and she is split—that is, detached—from the feeling aspect of the event, the very pitch, tone, timbre, and emotional expressiveness of the therapist's voice in replying can actually resonate with the deadened feeling and help bring it to the surface.

To illustrate, not from a therapeutic point of view, but simply that of a feeling human being, let me offer a story from my own life. About ten years ago I was admitted to the hospital on an emergency basis for diagnostic tests. I was sitting in a hospital bed, wearing a hospital gown, when a female resident came in to take my personal and familial medical history. As we worked our way through the myriad of questions, her presentation was professional, with a smooth bedside manner. We had been talking for about ten minutes when she asked me a question about my parents' general health. I answered that my father was healthy, so far as I knew, but that my mother had died about seven years before. She looked up from her note taking and said in a warm, sincere tone, "I'm so sorry." Then she went back to her notes. In that moment, a feeling of sadness at my mother's death welled up in a way that had not happened in many years. To my complete surprise, tears sprang to my eyes. When my mother died all those years before I had availed myself of the help to be had in feeling and had grieved deeply and heavily. By the time of this incident, though I still thought of my mother frequently, it was without any of that tearing sense of grief. Though of course I was concerned and anxious at being admitted to the hospital, I was not aware of any underlying state of sadness. It wasn't until later that I realized that the last time I had been in a hospital room was as my mother lay dying. So, what had just happened there?

Through her accidental use of what I call *voice mirroring* the training physician helped bring up my feeling. It was not only her words, but her tone of warmth, compassion, and sorrow that reverberated within my emotional memory. When a person is disconnected from her feeling by time, distance, or repression, a therapist's use of voice will often help reunite those split-off elements of her experience. This effect does not happen in response to a concerted effort to sound sympathetic and caring because if there is any effort involved, the response will be false and have little or no effect on the other person's emotional state, except to make her wonder why the therapist is trying so hard to make it sound as if he cares. I am speaking of allowing one's natural response to arise and be expressed in the voice. If a patient is telling of a painful event in her life and the therapist's questions and responses are offered in a voice that is not congruent with what is being told, this can naturally have a chilling effect on any emotion the person may be experiencing. Conversely, the opposite is true, especially with someone who is severely out of touch with her own feelings. Having someone respond in an open and spontaneous way can have the effect of arousing her emotions, leaving her more open to a deepening of those same feelings. For most of the patients with whom I work, receiving such a response is not the norm. Frequently they have been ridiculed, hit, and punished for letting any vulnerable emotion show. They naturally can often find it very difficult to reveal what they feel *even to themselves*, much less to a stranger, such as myself. To reiterate, in voice mirroring the voice of the therapist reflects the deeper emotion that the patient has buried, denied, forgotten, or simply is not in touch with for the moment.

Another way in which voice is helpful is in setting the tone of the session. When a patient with whom I am working comes to therapy in an avoidant mode, chattering and racing in what I can see are not just ordinary good spirits, which I would support, but in an attempt to deny and avoid his present internal emotional reality, I try to help the patient "drop down a level" by speaking and asking my questions in a fully present, aware tone. When the patient is trying to rise above what he feels, dropping down often leads to an immediate awareness of whatever emotion he is running from. I particularly see this defensive behavior when patients need to confront me about something I have said or done that frightens or angers them. I also see this when they are contemplating revealing something that is especially painful or about which they feel a great deal of shame.

In Part One of this book, readers were undoubtedly struck by the number of places where, instead of dialogue, there is only the word SILENCE. I did this to indicate what I consider, at times, to be a tool more important than any intervention a therapist can make, particularly when working with deep emotions. It is frequently in the moments of silence in a session that buried feelings begin to come to the surface. It can happen after a powerful question has been asked, or after the patient has had an insight or intense realization. If interrupted at these crucial moments, he may be denied the opportunity to touch as deeply as he might feelings and insights that have long been buried. It is in recognizing the quality of a particular silence that a therapist's experience, insight, and intuition come into play. For although it might be appropriate for a silence that is deepening to last for minutes, it can also be a waste of precious time—if, for example, the silence is only continuing because the patient or therapist is confused, withholding, or falling asleep. I usually make it a point to remain silent after a person has been crying, unless it is clear to me that he needs some assistance or encouragement to continue the feeling. I maintain the silence at these moments because I know that this is very frequently a time when insight is arising or the patient is making internal connections to other events that relate to what he has been crying about. Thus, another aspect of silence in a session is timing. There are moments when it is important to speak almost immediately and others when a long period of silence is what will be of the most help in opening the patient to his inner emotional world. Examples of all these techniques appear in the therapy sessions that preceded this section of this work.

Termination

THE NATURAL FLOW OF A COURSE OF THERAPY
includes a point when it is time to end. Depending
on the level of pain a patient is carrying when he enters therapy, as well as the goals he has, therapy can
last from as little as one year to seven years and beyond. I consider that the therapy has served its purpose when it is obvious to me and to the patient that
he or she functions better in daily life, feels better
about him or herself, is able to be in touch with emotions, is able to handle change constructively, can accept challenges and responsibilities, and is no longer
controlled by past trauma. Another indicator that we
are approaching the end of therapy is that the sense
of need for therapy decreases. The patient begins to
generally feel that she can handle the crises of daily
life that arise, that the strengths and skills that she
has developed are equal to the tasks at hand. Sometimes patients will resist accepting this reality. It can
be difficult for all of us at times to take full responsibility for our lives. This, too, is worked through in the
termination phase of therapy.

Termination is a process in which patient and
therapist continue their work together with the goal
of having the ending be an enriching and enlivening

experience. Since few of the patients I have worked with in therapy have had positive endings to relationships in the past, this period of therapy can be an extremely stressful one, with the patient having periods of intense fears of abandonment and loss. Often regressive and acting-out behaviors that have not been part of therapy for years reappear. This period is usually short-lived due to the work that has already been done, but can at times be dramatic, sometimes bringing up feelings that therapy has been a waste of time because the thought of parting becomes so difficult. I must admit that the difficulty is not all on the patient's part; I, too, as a therapist must confront feelings of loss and sadness at the end of a connection that has been intense and full of feeling, and is of long standing.

Ideally the patient brings up the subject of termination and I have found it is usually an easier process if the patient is the one who initiates this discussion. Sometimes I have asked a question about how the patient is handling life in general, or whether his or her goals of therapy have basically been met, as an opening into the subject. Though occasionally a patient has decided to terminate before what I consider to be the optimum time, I feel that once I have expressed my concerns, it is his or her decision. One of the goals that I consistently work toward is for each person that I see as a patient to become her *own* person, to have an internal sense of what is right or wrong for her without undue reference to the overbearing opinions of others, including my own. One of my patients expressed it as no longer being buffeted by the winds of others' opinions, blown back and forth, here and there, but rather having the ability to sail steadily on her true course.

The other feelings that come up for patients during the termination process are ones of joy and relief that finally they no longer feel the need to come to therapy! Fear and guilt feelings—that they are leaving me behind and going on to live a separate life—come up as well. These feelings can be particularly powerful for the patient whose family was an entwining, consuming one and for those patients who have had a difficult ending with another therapist.

Once the decision to terminate has been reached, my patient and I work together to develop a schedule, gradually tapering the number of times we meet, finally picking a date that will be our last session. This last session can bring a tumult of emotions, running the gamut from joy and satisfaction to flashes of sorrow and rage. I make it clear that I have an open-door policy and that patients are free to call or schedule an appointment if they feel the need in the future. But finally this session, too, ends and we say good-bye, and go on to our now separate lives. This is a bittersweet moment, but one which we have worked for from the beginning.

As my final point I would like to say that crying is a natural human response to physical and emotional pain. In the best of all possible worlds, no one would have to come to therapy to regain the ability to cry. This capability is just as much a part of a person as being able to fall asleep when one is tired. The loss of either of those abilities is a sign that something has gone seriously wrong. Our society denigrates and has contempt for the tears of children. With this contempt the child's ability to be compassionate to himself and others is defeated or destroyed, leading to the plague of violence that haunts our society today. May this soon end.